THE VACCAI PROJECT

THE VACCAI PROJECT

Refine your technique.
Unlock your imagination.

A practice diary exploring
historically informed performance practice
of the bel canto style inspired by
the classic lessons of Vaccai

Rachelle Jonck and Derrick Goff

TABLE OF CONTENTS

TABLE OF CONTENTS

TABLE OF CONTENTS

TABLE OF CONTENTS

ACKNOWLEDGMENTS

Thank you to every singer, coach, teacher, pianist, conductor and opera fan who took part in The Vaccai Project since March of 2020. When we were isolating in New York City, the two constant things in our daily lives were banging on our pots and pans at 7:00 each night and writing the next day's Facebook post. Many days the sadness of Covid made it hard to write, but in the end **The Vaccai Project** was the "life raft we clung to" exactly like one singer described it to us. A special thank you to those of who became members of **Bel Canto Boot Camp** and every other member. Your support, financial and otherwise, made this project possible.

A big shout out to BCBC mentors and members who were so generous with their time, both during the initial creation of the course and the finalizing of the book. A special thank you to Dave Ekstrum, Nicholas Simpson, Timothy Cheung, Kimberly Gratland James, and Jennifer Moore. Thank you also to Hans Bridger Heruth who worked tirelessly with us to engrave Vaccai's lessons and to Nick Scholl who played an important role in the start of Bel Canto Boot Camp.

Steven Tharp's contribution to BCBC cannot be overstated. His **Guided by Voices** series and ongoing **Bel Canto Sunday Matinées** are an all important part of our work. His inspiration can be found all through this book.

Will Crutchfield has been an invaluable mentor, colleague, and friend to both of us. His wealth of knowledge has contributed so much to the information we present to you here. You will meet him virtually in the course of this book and we thank him for his generous input.

Thank you also to Lucy Tucker Yates for sharing much inspiration, insight, and love of the Italian libretto and language.

A big thank you to Rachelle's mom, Tersia, who put us up during the first months of putting together this book. Being in the African sun definitely made the daily grind of finding the "look of the book" and it's umpteenth edit a pleasure. She taught Rachelle to read music when she was three and continued to teach piano and lead her school's choir until age 79. She is an inspiration to us every day.

*Dedicated to the unquenchable human spirit
that shines so brightly in New York City.*

*Even in the face of unspeakable loss and challenge
it marches purposefully forward.*

Rachelle Derrick

Introduction

On March 12th, 2020, the unthinkable happened: The Metropolitan Opera closed its doors as New York buckled down for its extended battle with COVID-19. It was clear even in those early days of quarantine that we were entering trying times for the performing arts, inextricably dependent both on the ability of performers to meet in rehearsal and for artist and audience to meet in the concert hall or opera house. Of course this blow was particularly devastating for the acoustic performing arts where microphones and electronic speakers intrude on the directness of sound from unamplified voice to ear.

On March 16th we launched an online practice diary to provide community and inspiration for the singers we regularly work with in New York. It was designed to provide singers virtually with what ballet barre class delivers to dancers: a systematic exploration and practice of the basics of their technique. All too often, singers "warm up" and then try to fine-tune their technique by obsessively practicing (aka beating to death!) their repertoire. No more of that! Let's get back to basics and practice the skills of the bel canto technique with the help of the well-known lesson book of Nicola Vaccai – like ballet dancers daily maintain and refine their *plié, echappé,* and *port de bras.* **The Vaccai Project** was born! The Facebook group exploded as just short of 2,000 singers from around the world sang Vaccai together. Extended lockdowns world-wide inspired us to slow down and delve into details. We had the one thing we never have: TIME. Since then, our COVID project turned into **Bel Canto Boot Camp**, and **The Vaccai Project** was offered virtually an additional three times - each time with a blend of returning and new singers. In the virtual world our New York community could reach artists all over the world, breaking the often prohibitive barriers of distance, cost, time, and audition-only programs. We heard new voices from across the world, celebrated outstanding progress and achievement among participants, and experimented with new formats and modes of instruction. We pushed ourselves to codify what it is we believe and teach by putting it on screen.

So, why a book? Printing **The Vaccai Project** brings us back to a physical world where a singer can sit at a piano and work (or as we like to call it, play!) No screens. No microphones. No speakers. No pop-up messages. No distractions. Additionally a printed page often helps you create a visual image of information that is impossible to achieve with hyperlinks. It jolts the memory in the best possible way - you remember what you saw where. And when you write on it yourself, that effect is multiplied. Grab your pencil!

Most modern music books are either scores or textbooks. Maybe the score has an Introduction or Appendix with information in tiny print. Do you study it? Most textbooks have some score examples, but not enough to use in your every day practice. Historical treatises often have both but can be impossibly long and difficult to read. This book solves the problem: we combine the Vaccai score with our BCBC and historic exercises and essays on history and performance practice all together in one place. And while we're at it, you do some Italian libretto study as well! At Bel Canto Boot Camp, the pillars of our approach are **SING – READ – LISTEN**. We pin down the all-important listening portion through QR codes that allow you to put sound to text. A book with gorgeous sounds! What could be better?!

We present you with facts on singing in "the old bel canto style" that we consider undisputed – at least in the historical treatises – even if they might be controversial now. Not all evidence can be presented on the first day or even the first week or month – such is the business of teaching. **Try not to jump ahead. It is written to be read and practiced in order.** Resist the urge to say: "Oh, this is easy, let me skip to page 77." We are here fostering the habit of practicing basics – showing up for daily barre like dancers do. To understand that the basics of our craft is the foundation of our art. You will see that we repeat core principles often and try to explain them in different ways. Pick the language that works for you to remember and make your own.

Spend some quality time on the Daily Exercises chapters, but don't get stuck. These are exercises you will do every day for the rest of your life. The goal is NOT that you do them perfectly (though the more you do them, the closer you'll get!). The goal is that you do it! **Perfection is unattainable.**

Once you start the lessons, move at your own pace but keep going - but don't rush! The course was conceived as daily practice inspiration - don't do more than one chapter per day - and don't skip using the Practice Journal. It will help you both celebrate your victories and work through the tough times. Take time to internalize and above all, practice and apply the information. Take breaks as needed to synthesize the information, but remember that skill building depends on consistency of practice. Accomplish your tasks with a positive and joyful attitude. There is room for multiple diary entries per chapter to inspire you to move through the course multiple times. Don't paralyze yourself by self-judgment. Keep moving forward - you will come down this road again! Singers and teachers just like you repeated this course back to back during Covid. Every single one of them commented on how evident their growth was to them when they came back to a lesson for a second, third and fourth time. You can do this!

A note about Daily Exercises: Many historic exercise books start with preparatory exercises to prepare the singer for more complicated vocalises. The first five chapters of our book follow this model. The most elementary exercise executed with superior skill is a thing of beauty to behold. That holds true for the prima ballerina's *port de bras* and the prima donna's *legato*.

The chapters on *Messa di voce* and *Laryngeal Registration* are aimed at more advanced singers. If you are new to these skills, feel free to skip these chapters up front. You can go back to them after Lesson 4 where Vaccai will help you develop these skills.

A note about the practice sheets: We decided to keep the practice sheets in their original often handwritten form. We are sentimental about them! Rachelle got better at using her iPad and ForScore as she went along. And then we discovered Canva and Derrick helped her to get more creative yet! But essentially they are home-made. Some people baked bread during Covid, Rachelle wrote out exercises! On our website they live on the color coded Gym Floor - our practice platform with separate stations for Daily Exercises, Ornamentation, Registration, Italian, Singer's Mindset, etc. They are designed to be fun and keep you in a playful mood. We learn when we play.

A note about voice science: Our book includes some very basic references to voice science, which are in no way designed to be a beginner's guide to this great discipline. Most singers do better when technique is de-mystified by some simple facts that can easily be applied in practice. Most also become incapacitated when too many complicated concepts crowd their minds while they sing. We aim to help you strike a balance. We keep it simple, practical and playful. Just go with the flow! Think, but don't over-think.

A note about sport psychology: Rachelle is a huge sports fan - Derrick not so much! But we are both fans of the sport psychologist Bob Rotella. His book *Golf Is Not a Game of Perfect* is a gold mine. It does not teach you NOT to think - it teaches you HOW to think and stay focused. Singers must think. Theirs is an art of incredible finesse requiring minute attention to detail. With Bob's help we show you ways to allow your body and mind to work together without sabotaging each other.

A note about the Vaccai lessons: Our edition of the lessons is not meant to be a critical edition of the original book, but is geared towards performance and understanding of the historical notational language of the bel canto era. Specific choices are explained lesson by lesson - here are some general ones:

- We capitalize the first letter of each poetic line as it appears in the original libretti to keep you firmly rooted in your Italian poetry study. Vowels that go together in one syllable are indicated by an undertie (presso‿al). We provide diction help by indicating open and closed vowels.
- We conform to old-fashioned vocal notational practice by placing a slur over all notes that occur on a single syllable. We also beam together all notes within a beat that belong on one syllable. We are doing everything in our power to help you see one syllable where you might be tempted to see two (or even three!) You will soon discover that poetry is a priority here!

We print the lessons in the "medium key" - they are available in both a higher and lower key and in bass clef on our website at **belcantobootcamp.com/vaccai**; sing them in any key, of course!

Venturing beyond the lessons: Vaccai inspired us to go beyond his pages - to explore all the HIPP (historically informed performance practice) they hint at. We hope you will enjoy taking these excursions with us. Yes, they make our journey longer, but like any truly leisurely and memorable trip, it allows us to feel we really explored the surroundings and made it our own.

A note about historic terminology: We will often quote from classic historical treatises. During the period we are exploring there was no general consensus on "what to call what". One man's mordent was another man's turn! Our purpose here will be to comprehend and practice the *notes* the theorists are describing, not to get bogged down by the study of the evolution of terminology, as fascinating as it may be. Practicality is the name of the game here. We use symbols and color-coding to keep us all focused on our mutual goals: exploring history to help you be the very best singer you can be, while keeping the mind crystal clear.

You will see us refer to our website from time to time. Not everything we developed in the last couple of years can be printed! We invite you to use this QR code to join our online community. First three months' membership on us!

Let's get started!
Rachelle and Derrick

belcantobootcamp.com
Contact us at belcantobootcamp@gmail.com

Daily Exercises: One Note

Growing as a singer starts with singing one note. Seriously! As evidence we present the first lessons from Marchesi, Mengozzi and Cinti-Damoreau's treatises. Singers should start their day with onset and long note exercises. There is a good reason historic exercise books start with one note and not a nine tone scale. **One note, one vowel** is how you find your consistent free flowing air – the holy grail of bel canto. Or, as we call it here:

ONE BREATH IMPULSE PER PHRASE

For some singers it is easier to start with multiple onsets on one note in one breath impulse, for example, four shorter notes and then one long one. Or three if you are in a waltzy mood! How do I sing multiple onsets in one breath impulse? If you laugh, you are executing multiple onsets in one breath impulse. Unless you are laughing like Santa Claus with a bouncing belly! Not like that. Do you need to put H's to get the idea? Go ahead. Then take them out because there are no H's in Italian! *(Opinion: No practicing audible glottal attacks here, because there are no glottals in Italian diction. Yes, glottal closure is essential for clean onset, but too often singers overreach in this department and it results in a scoop from a non-defined lower pitch. So inelegant! We are looking for your very best coordinated onset you study with your teacher.)*

this exercise can be done on any vowel,
but should definitely be practiced on /a/

Now go back to executing a single attack and sustaining the note in a solid dynamic. This is Manuel García's *force égale* (equal dynamic) – his first kind of *sons soutenus* (sustained tones) that he discusses in his treatise. Goal is to start right on the pitch with vibrato on a vowel without a strong discernible glottal (see above). No scooping! Practice all your vowels and make sure that someone else would know what they are if they were listening. You can just pick and sing any notes. Nobody says it must be a scale. Sometimes it is fun to just pick a pitch with your ear and sing it. Get away from the keyboard. Sing in the shower. Sing while doing the dishes. Sit on a balance ball. Lie on the floor.

WHEREVER YOU SING' EM, SING' EM LONG!
GET HAPPY ON THAT NOTE!

Let your breath flow! If you keep singing them without thinking about it too much you will hit a groove and get happy.

Sports psychologist and author Bob Rotella teaches his golf students (and golf pros!) to "look at the target, look at the ball, let it go." **Imagine the pitch and the vowel, take a breath, let it go.** LONG note. DON'T JUDGE. Keep doing it. The same way. Different pitch, different vowel, breathe, let it go. Pitch/vowel, breathe, go! Try to get a cycle of breath going where each breath produces a tone. No extra breaths in between. No thinking. No judging your attack and restarting. Target, breathe, go LOOOOOONNGG, target, breathe, go LOOOOOOOOONNNNGGG.

Marchesi, *Vocal Method*, Op. 31 (1887)

If you don't know Bob Rotella's *Golf Is Not a Game of Perfect*, you should get to know it sooner rather than later! It is by far the best sports psychology book I know. It does not tell you to STOP THINKING. Instead it teaches you HOW TO THINK. Singers by nature are thinkers – trying to stop thinking is futile. Learn to control your thoughts.

LEARNING FROM SPORTS PSYCHOLOGY

CHOOSING HOW TO THINK

- Your potential depends primarily on your attitude, how well you sing, and how well you think.
- A singer can and must decide how to think.
- Courage is a necessary quality in all champions. But a singer cannot be courageous without first being afraid.

THINKING CONSISTENTLY

- The foundation of good singing is a good pre-sing routine.
- To sing consistently a singer must think consistently.
- It's more important to be decisive than to be correct.
- Acceptance is the last step in a sound routine.

PRACTICING TO TRUST

- To improve, you must practice. But the quality of your practice is more important than the quantity, particularly for advanced singers.
- You must train yourself in physical technique and then practice trusting what was trained.
- You must spend at least 60 percent of your practice time in the trusting mentality.
- On the first phrase of the role you must expect only two things from yourself: to have fun, and to focus your mind properly.

adapted from Bob Rotella, Golf Is Not a Game of Perfect

Mengozzi, *Méthode de chant du Conservatoire de Musique à Paris* (1803)

Don't push the range issue. Sing only the notes you can sing without straining your voice. While Cinti-Damoreau's two octaves (below) are the goal, we don't need to achieve that immediately. For the purposes of Vaccai you are only going to sing the pitches you can sing comfortably in any case.

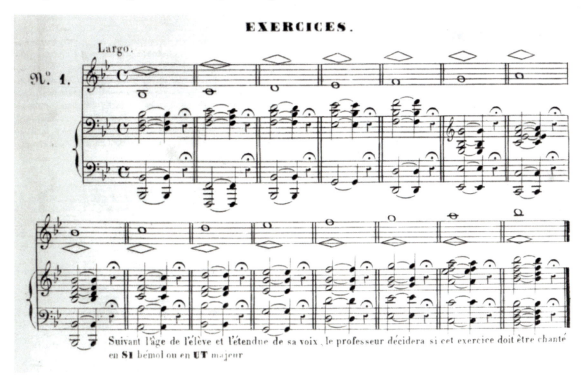

Cinti-Damoreau, *Méthode de chant* (1849)

Manuel García (1805, Madrid—1906, London) was the son of the famous tenor bearing the same name, often referred to as García Père (father). García, baritone and author of the *Complete Treatise on the Art of Singing*, debuted at age 20 in New York as Figaro in his father's production of *Il barbiere di Siviglia*, but a few years later abandoned his operatic career, having returned to Paris, where he had studied. After completing military service in Algiers, García undertook administrative duties in hospitals in France, where he studied the physiology and anatomy of the voice, eventually inventing the first laryngoscope in 1855. García's most famous students included Jenny Lind, Mathilde Marchesi, and Julius Stockhausen. After teaching at the Paris Conservatoire, he eventually taught from 1848-1895 at the Royal Academy of Music in London. He died in England at the age of 101.

Manuel García
at the age of 100
original image: Archivio Storico Ricordi

Practice Journal

_____ , 20 ___

_____

_____

_____

_____

_____

_____ , 20 ___

_____

_____

_____

_____

_____

_____ , 20 ___

_____

_____

_____

_____

_____

IF YOU FEEL CONFIDENT IN ONE NOTE AT ONE DYNAMIC, PRACTICE THE CLASSIC BEL CANTO EXERCISE - MESSA DI VOCE

Let us explore the chest voice/head voice balance possibilities throughout your range. Too many modern singers skip *messa di voce* (García's second kind of sustained tone, or *son filé*). While dynamics result in a "color", they are achieved by being in control of your laryngeal registration. All the old treatises and exercise books talk about *messa di voce* as an exercise "to blend the registers."

EVERY NOTE IS "MIXED" OR "BLENDED"

- Every classically produced **chest-dominant** note still involves participation of the head voice (CT remains engaged.)

- The floatiest high note in classically produced **head-dominant** head voice still involves participation of the chest voice (TA remains engaged.)

You may see the following terms which refer to the same things:
chest voice, modal voice, thick folds, thyroarytenoid (TA) dominance, "mix", Mode 1 (M1)

head voice, loft, thin folds, cricothyroid (CT) dominance, "mix", Mode 2 (M2)

You will see that we include "mix" in both categories since singers will use that term to refer to both their "heady chest" when they are in M1 and "chesty head" when they are in M2. Much confusion stems from this and thus we tend to avoid the term all together! **Let's not call some things "mixed" if everything is "mixed"!**

The goal is to start in a supported piano, make a gradual crescendo (shifting towards a chestier blend) and then a gradual diminuendo (shifting to a headier blend). Sometimes it is easier to start at *mp* to make sure you are not starting "off the voice." Stop within the range of beauty – this is bel canto! The important thing is to gain control of your dynamics while supporting your voice - maintaining **one breath impulse per phrase**. If you can control your midrange dynamics the rest will come with practice. Have patience! Give yourself time!

Domenico Corri describes *messa di voce* as "the soul of music." I would take it a step further. When you show the full range of available blends on a note you bare your very own soul. You show all there is to show. There is no place to hide in a *messa di voce*.

It requires both flawless technique and a brave spirit to reveal your true voice.

Corri, *The Singer's Preceptor* (1810)

Become the MVP of the MDV is BCBC's guide to this classic exercise. Our rocking horse helps you visualize the chest/head balance. More about registration and dynamics in Daily Exercises: Laryngeal Registration on the website. This QR code accesses a coaching video exploring long tones and messa di voce.

Spend the day singing one note at a time throughout your comfortable range of both pitch and dynamic. No crooning! No pushing!

START EVERY DAY OF THE REST OF YOUR LIFE THIS WAY.

Singing long notes is where you grow confidence.

Messa di voce is where you expand your color palette.

1. Do one thing at a time:

    a) Garaudé: "Sing sustained tones in different dynamics - ONE dynamic at a time."

    b) Panofka: "First crescendo - take a breath - then diminuendo."

2. Ask a neighbor for help:

    a) Bordèse: "Try changing the pitch at the apex of your crescendo?"

BCBC suggestion: Repeat with whole steps. Improve messa di voce and legato in small intervals all at the same time!

    b) Celoni: "Let's get a longer breath going and sustain the apex of the crescendo."

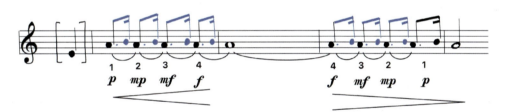

BCBC in blue: Use upper neighbor tones to help you define mid-level dynamics. Then leave out the blue notes!

3. The BCBC way:

    Work outwards from your best mid-level (mezzo-piano) dynamic.

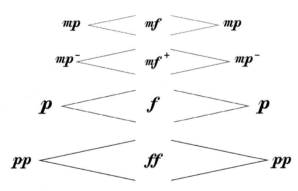

soprano and mezzo-soprano voices
F4 and above in M1

soprano and mezzo-soprano voices between C4 and F4

soprano and mezzo-soprano voices
C4 and below
tenor, baritone, and bass voices
through the range in M2

ff and pp are not absolute terms; what do they represent as your voice changes and develops? as you refine your skills?

Since the pitches between C4 and F4 can be achieved both in M1 and M2 your MDV on these pitches can span both laryngeal vibratory modes

References:
Garaudé, *Méthode complète de chant* (1854)
Pellegrini Celoni, *Grammatica* (1810)
Bordèse, *Méthode élémentaire du chant* (1852)
Panofka, *L'art de chanter, op. 81* (1854)

Practice Journal

———————————— , 20 —

_____

_____

_____

_____

_____

———————————— , 20 —

_____

_____

_____

_____

———————————— , 20 —

_____

_____

_____

_____

_____

_____

where do you need great
long notes and messa di voce
in your repertoire?

_____

_____

_____

_____

_____

_____

It is time to connect some glorious pitches to each other! Remember to continue to practice your onsets and long notes every day - these are **Daily Exercises**. Don't skip any of them ever.

I am often asked if *legato* and *portamento* are the same thing; they are not. (In a later chapter we will share some historical quotes on the subject. For now you are going to explore in your own throat what true legato feels like.)

LEGATO

is a musical term meaning "smoothly bound together
without breaks between the notes."

PORTAMENTO

is how a singer achieves this.

A lot of confusion stems from some pianists' inexperience making this distinction. When pianists desire legato as a musical goal, they have ten fingers to achieve it. Simply put, a pianist puts down note B before releasing note A to achieve what we call "finger legato." Singers cannot sing two notes at the same time. Of course pianists also have a sustain pedal to "bind notes together" if the fingers cannot reach. Singers have no such pedal. The pianist feigns legato – the notes are bound together by allowing them slightly to overlap. I choose the piano here because the vast majority of musicians (other than singers) working with and talking to singers are pianists.

In a similar way we can think about other instruments. The string player can put down a second finger on the fingerboard before picking up the first one. BUT he has an option the pianist does not have: he can slide! One finger on one string: to make two notes legato the finger can slide and it results in a *portamento* if the bow stays connected to the string. We hear the two notes and everything in between them. Interestingly enough, string players used to play with more portamento when singers sang with more. Not surprising, since basically every instrumentalist is trying to make his instrument SING. A very basic outline of why singers stopped singing with "so much portamento" can be found in a side bar on the next page. An exploration of all the reasons would require a separate book!

We know string players played with more portamento because they were taught to do it in their own exercise books and the survival of written-in fingerings shows how often in performance they favored the less obvious choice in order to achieve truly 'smoothly bound together' notes.

See below an example from Dotzauer's 1826 *Violonzellschule* (section titled "Das Ziehen von einem Ton zum andern" – "Sliding from one pitch to another")

Back to singers! Since we don't have fingers and pedals, what are we to do?! Since breath is how we make sound we obviously cannot interrupt our air flow, thus our mantra:

ONE BREATH IMPULSE PER PHRASE

If we change the length of our vocal folds while keeping our breath engaged, we hear what the Italians call *portamento*. It is just how the instrument works. Ain't no other way to get there unless you interrupt your air flow (oops! now you are no longer singing legato) or separate the pitches in some other muscular way, for example with your jaw (oops! now you are no longer binding together smoothly). While portamento is not the goal – legato is – portamento is the result of truly consistent breath between the pitches. Call it "support" or "cheesecake" if the word portamento scares you. Just do it!

All the old treatises follow onset and *messa di voce* exercises with portamento. We should too. Excerpts are from Marchesi – semitone and tones and some bigger intervals if you feel like it. At BCBC we often just sing legato semitones and tones up and down from different pitches (pick pitches while showering or lying on the floor just like you did with your one note exercises). We call it "flossing" since it is something you should do every day. I'm serious.

YOU MUST PRACTICE PORTAMENTO EVERY DAY

practice on all vowels, especially /a/

Change pitches without interrupting your air (support). It seems pretty basic, but do you do it? In all your small intervals? On "Dove **so**no"? On "Ach, **ich fühl's**, es ist **ver**schwunden"? "Il mio te**soro intan**to"? "Der Vogel**fänger** bin ich ja"? Amazing that all the examples that popped in my head are Mozart...if you think Mozart should not be sung legato, think again.

Can you commit to singing all your tones and semitones legato? There are a lot of them in your repertoire! **Your improved legato line starts right here: when you realize just how many small intervals you sing without care – without true legato.** This QR code links to a BCBC coaching video on Two Note Exercises.

Why did singers stop singing with "so much portamento"?

A down and dirty answer lies somewhere between the arrival of the microphone and the falling out of fashion of the melismatic styles. One note per syllable, aka all pitches introduced by consonants in the late romantic German repertoire and the Italian verismo eventually allowed singers to get lazy about practicing their scales. Note that the singers who debuted that repertoire were all still trained in the classic bel canto tradition. (Later generations of singers have not always been that lucky.) The simultaneous arrival of the microphone and subsequent development of amplification created a perfect storm: now singers (and orators) could truly get away without supporting their voices between pitches - the sound was no longer carried directly from voice to ear. Electronics got in the way. They still do!

where in your repertoire do you miss the opportunity to sing beautiful legato whole and half steps?

_____

_____

_____

_____

_____

18

Chromatic Slur.

Clarify your goal:

CHANGE THE PITCH WHILE MAINTAINING CONSISTENT SUPPORT

Marchesi, *Vocal Method, Op. 31* (1887)

Diatonic Slur.

Stay focused:
COMMIT TO SINGING SMALL INTERVALS LEGATO

Marchesi, *Vocal Method, Op. 31* (1887)

Portamento.

Remember our mantra:
ONE BREATH IMPULSE PER PHRASE

Marchesi, *Vocal Method, Op. 31* (1887)

Practice Journal

_____ , 20 __

_____

_____

_____

_____

_____

_____

_____ , 20 __

_____

_____

_____

_____

_____

_____

_____ , 20 __

_____

_____

_____

_____

_____

_____

Advanced: Laryngeal Registration

For an advanced challenge, explore transitioning between your laryngeal registers during your two note exercises. Historical treatises are in agreement that singers should be trained to sing calmly ("without forcing" in the words of Pauline Viardot) in chest voice up to F4. A number of theorists, including Garaudé and Mengozzi, exercise pitches up to G4 in chest. We share these to impart that up to F4 in chest was not considered extreme.

From a practical perspective, stick to Viardot's suggestion of F4 as the pivot point between chest and head dominance.

Look at Viardot's exercise on the next page. Sopranos and mezzo-sopranos can also explore the low pitches in head voice (as low as comfortable) even if you will not sing them thus in public. It will help you find a myriad of colors in your chest voice. **Chest voice is not only for singing forte!** Remember our *messa di voce* chapter?

CONTROL OF DYNAMIC IS CONTROL OF REGISTRATION

As an advanced soprano or mezzo-soprano, can you sing a legato interval from E4 to F♯4 and back, transitioning smoothly, maintaining the same dynamic – preferably not *forte*, from chest (dominance) to head (dominance) and back? Tenors, baritones, and basses should practice this transition with chest/falsetto switching even if in repertoire you will remain chest-dominant.

"Welcoming the head voice" in switching exercises will improve the non-treble voice's dynamic range around and above the laryngeal passaggio. Baritones, think of all Verdi's "dolce" requests on F4. Tenors, you'll find your B-flat 4 in piano as requested by Gounod and others. Facility in head-voice was considered integral to the training of non-treble voices. Too often nowadays this training is overlooked resulting in tenors, baritones and basses singing unsupported in the softer dynamics - that is if they attempt softer dynamics at all.

Pauline Viardot was an accomplished singer, pianist, and composer. She was the daughter of Manuel García (the tenor), sister of Manuel García (the baritone and treatise writer) and Maria Malibran, goddaughter of Paer, student of Liszt and Reicha, friend of Chopin and Georges Sand, and muse of Gounod who wrote Sapho for her. She had a tremendous influence on the composers of her time - Saint-Saëns, Berlioz, Meyerbeer, Fauré. Her famous salons were the meeting place of artists of all disciplines. Much of 19th century musical activity in Europe was connected to her. She was a fierce ambassador for our art and her influence cannot possibly be overstated.

> **Pro tip:** The chest-dominant E4 must have a lot of head voice in it to ensure smooth transition to the F#4 which is in "strong head voice." This smooth transition between thyroarytenoid- or TA-dominant (Mode 1) and cricothyroid- or CT-dominant production (Mode 2) is an advanced skill. We're talking here about switching from 51%-49% to 49%-51%. I know you don't have a dial, just play with the idea! Read Garaudé on the next page.

EVERY NOTE IS MIXED - **MIXED HOW** IS UP TO YOU

Don't be hard on yourself if you find this difficult – everybody does! **Repetition is the mother of skill.** Before you tell yourself "I am bad. I cannot do it!", ask yourself, "Have I tried consistently for long enough while insisting that I keep a positive attitude and have fun?" This is just the beginning of our journey.

For an even more advanced skill you can try to **transition on one pitch** like Mengozzi (1758 – 1800) suggests. He was a singer, composer and voice professor at the Paris Conservatory where he compiled the *Méthode de chant* (find it on *Bel Canto Bookshelf* on our website). Those were the days when a syllabus provided concise description **with exercises** of the skill set a singer needed to master in order to graduate. Now we seem mostly to list repertoire requirements. To this we've come...

Mengozzi, *Méthode de chant* (1804)

P is for *poitrine* (chest voice) and T is for *tête* (head voice). We will come back to this skill many times during this course. **Reminder:** We use the short hand "chest voice" when we mean chest-dominant production and "head voice" when we mean head-dominant production.

All well-produced tones are mixed.

24

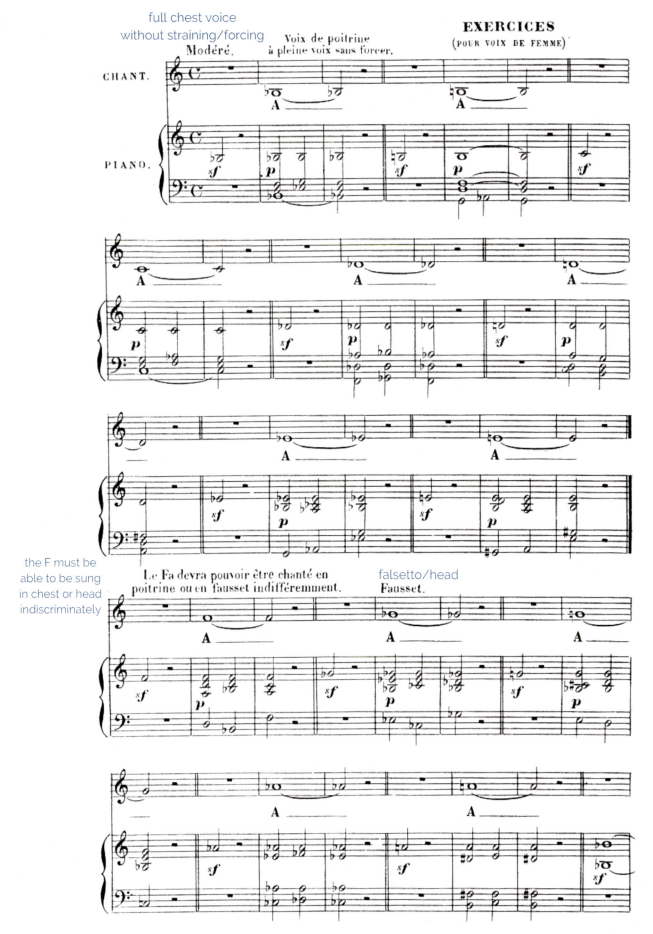

Viardot, *Une heure d'étude* (1897)

On the following pages are **Historical Switch Exercises** as well as our streamlined version. There are more registration exercises on the BCBC website. We will visit most of them one by one during this book so don't rush it!

Are you still maintaining your pre-sing routine? Keep it simple. Easier said than done, we know. But remember that these first chapters are about daily practice. There is no such thing as a perfect *plié* in barre class either – yet ballet dancers do them every day.

If the register transitions all the way to F4 are too advanced for you, take a step back. Be patient with yourself. You will be starting every day with these exercises – for the rest of your life!

You are becoming the master of your voice!

The perfect and imperceptible meeting of the different registers of the voice forms an essential part of the art of singing. One must avoid any type of toughness or hiccup that would result from the passage from one to the other. In some voices this passaggio is not very prominent; but in most others, this defect is only too frequent. The last note of chest-dominance and the first of head-dominance, or vice-versa, have to be connected naturally and effortlessly, in a manner that one would not notice the change. These exercises, when worked carefully, will give students the means to overcome this obstacle, and will make them to acquire the perfect equality of timbre that the Italians call voce spianata (leveled voice), that sets the best singers apart. **Garaudé on sopranos**

This voice has two registers: that of Chest and that of head. To pass easily from one to the other, one must sweeten the last note of the chest voice and strengthen the first of the head voice, as it is by nature weaker. In tenor voices, head voice used skillfully has infinite charm. One must commit to give it force, equality, purity, and to unify it imperceptibly with the chest voice. **Garaudé on tenors**

Alexis Adelaïde de Garaudé (1779-1852) was a French singer and composer, and a singing student of Crescentini, whose vocalises he published. He wrote his first Complete Vocal Method when he was teaching at the Paris Conservatoire in 1810. The first edition was printed in 1840.

Garcia starts his switching exercise here on a single pitch. This might work for you but it might make more sense for your voice to do these exercises in reverse order, starting with No. 4

Note how García sticks consistently to F4 as the highest note in "poitrine" (chest).

If a minor third is not large enough to get clarify the laryngeal tilt for you, extend to even larger intervals. We will encounter basic laryngeal exercises for the treble voice in Vaccai's lessons on sevenths and octaves.

sure qu'on les fait plus facilement, il faudra presser le mouvement jusqu'à ce qu'on puisse chanter d'une seule respiration le N.º 8. Il faudra faire attention de chanter jusqu'au Fa en voix de poitrine, tant en descendant qu'en montant.

Viardot: "One must take care to sing up until F in chest voice, both descending and ascending"

García, *Traité complet de l'art du chant* (1847), Viardot, *Une heure d'étude* (1897)

Garaudé for treble voices:

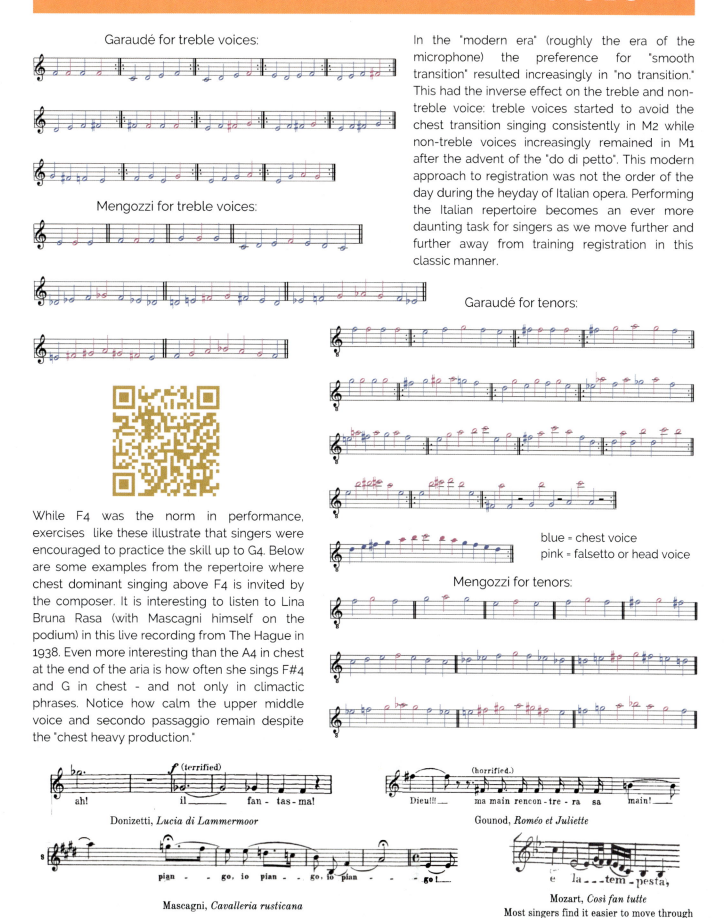

Mengozzi for treble voices:

In the "modern era" (roughly the era of the microphone) the preference for "smooth transition" resulted increasingly in "no transition." This had the inverse effect on the treble and non-treble voice: treble voices started to avoid the chest transition singing consistently in M2 while non-treble voices increasingly remained in M1 after the advent of the "do di petto". This modern approach to registration was not the order of the day during the heyday of Italian opera. Performing the Italian repertoire becomes an ever more daunting task for singers as we move further and further away from training registration in this classic manner.

Garaudé for tenors:

While F4 was the norm in performance, exercises like these illustrate that singers were encouraged to practice the skill up to G4. Below are some examples from the repertoire where chest dominant singing above F4 is invited by the composer. It is interesting to listen to Lina Bruna Rasa (with Mascagni himself on the podium) in this live recording from The Hague in 1938. Even more interesting than the A4 in chest at the end of the aria is how often she sings F#4 and G in chest - and not only in climactic phrases. Notice how calm the upper middle voice and secondo passaggio remain despite the "chest heavy production."

blue = chest voice
pink = falsetto or head voice

Mengozzi for tenors:

ah!   il _____ fan - tas - ma!

Donizetti, *Lucia di Lammermoor*

Dieu!!! _____ ma main rencon - tre - ra sa main!

Gounod, *Roméo et Juliette*

pian - - go, io pian - - go, io pian - - go!

Mascagni, *Cavalleria rusticana*

e la _ _ tem _ pesta,

Mozart, *Così fan tutte*
Most singers find it easier to move through
G4 staying in "light chest" in this passage

Garaudé, *Méthode complète de chant* (1854) Mengozzi, *Méthode complet* (1840)

BCBC SWITCH EXERCISES

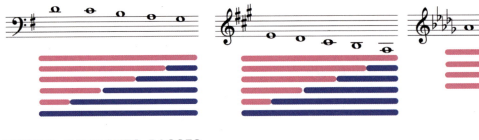

TENORS, BARITONES, BASSES

Sing this exercise in all keys in which you can sing all five pitches in easy falsetto as well as chest-dominant 'full voice'

blue = chest voice
pink = falsetto or head voice

SOPRANOS, MEZZO-SOPRANOS, CONTRALTOS

This exercise inspires you to practice transitioning on different pitches towards your eventual goal of achieving F4 equally easily in head or chest dominance. Start in a key where you can sing all five pitches in head voice and sing at least the lowest note in chest, progressing up to F major.

Non-treble voices

Take this exercise as high as your falsetto and full voice allow on the top note

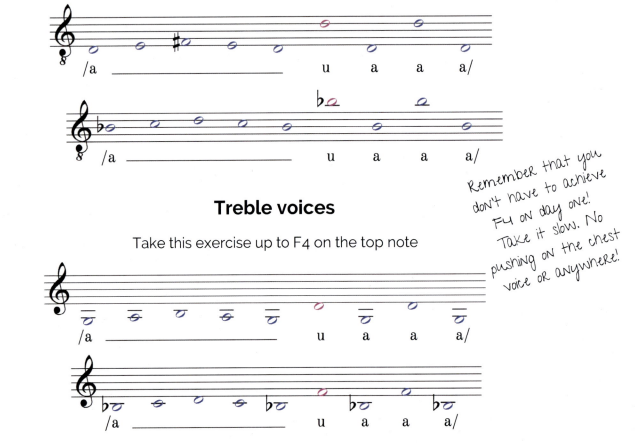

/a _____ u a a a/

/a _____ u a a a/

Treble voices

Take this exercise up to F4 on the top note

/a _____ u a a a/

/a _____ u a a a/

Remember that you don't have to achieve F4 on day one! Take it slow. No pushing on the chest voice or anywhere!

Practice Journal

_____ , 20 ___

_____

_____

_____

_____

_____

_____ , 20 ___

_____

_____

_____

_____

_____

_____ , 20 ___

_____

_____

_____

_____

_____

Daily Exercises: Consonants

Include consonants in your daily technical practice – ignoring them is a recipe for disaster and will leave you wondering why you sing better in the studio than on stage! It is not true, not even in Italian, that legato means "singing on the vowels as long as possible."

LEGATO IS CONTINUED BREATH, NOT CONTINUED VOWEL.

"Staying on the vowel as long as possible" is only true when the consonant is single and the vowel is long. A double consonant consequentially shortens the preceding vowel; it's up to you to coordinate keeping your breath impulse consistent through the sustained consonant time. Otherwise, bye-bye legato!

This is particularly important through the **sustainable voiced consonants M /m/, L /l/, N /n/, V /v/, R /r/, and NG /ŋ/.** You can practice your sustained voiced consonants by making them part of the one note and two note exercises we've been doing. Try oscillating between one vowel and a consonant (A-M-A-M-A, O-L-O-L-O, etc) while concentrating on:

> a) keeping the breath consistent (continued pitch and vibrato)
> b) keeping the larynx in the same position as the vowel while on the consonant
> c) moving the jaw only when necessary (keep that jaw from closing on L, N and NG which are made by ONLY moving the tongue; and move the jaw as little as possible for M, V and R)

My people, let us try not to get side tracked here! For purposes of DOING instead of TALKING or THINKING, just be conscious that your laryngeal position stays the same – wherever you and your teacher believe it is – when you move to and from your consonants. We at BCBC tend to refer to desired laryngeal position in classical singing as "low neutral" but I don't want to get into that can of worms deeper than I have to!

People will tell you not to "chew your consonants."
While it is true that excessive movement of the jaw is a bad idea,
clenching your throat and raising your larynx
while producing your consonants is worse, or at least as bad!

Sing a nice long AAAAAA-MMMMMM-AAAAAAAA. Don't change anything that must not change to get to MMMMMM. I call M "hot french fry"! Keep your vowel space and close your lips around it. No clenching of the teeth and the throat. Hear how resonant that consonant becomes if you give the poor thing some space to spin! Repeat with all the other sustainable voiced consonants.

Always start with the vowel first to find your position, then consonant, back and forth. Keep it slow! This QR code links you to a video discussing sustainable voiced consonants in detail.

You can also practice not changing your breath flow (and laryngeal position... you get my drift by now?!) on **F /f/, S /s/, and SH /ʃ/ (unvoiced fricatives)** with the same oscillation exercise. You'd be surprised how easy it is to grab your throat on those consonants – especially if your character is going through a tough time. Maybe her brother insisted that she marry someone she doesn't want to marry. Lucia had better keep her throat open in that mad scene!

While you're at it, go through the alphabet and feel what all the other consonants feel like if you pop them in your oscillation exercise.

P /p/, T /t/, and K /k/ are the axis of evil! They are the only consonants that interrupt air flow and ain't a thing any of us can do about it! Especially when they are double, be sure to "suspend the air" calmly without (yes you guessed it!) grabbing your throat. Try not to explode the air when you go back to your vowel. Because a) they are not plosives in Italian and b) it is a bad idea if your goal is continued spin and dynamic, also known as good legato line!

Their voiced counterparts **B /b/, D /d/, and G /g/** are tricky as well. DON'T grab your throat! **Always start with the vowel**, then go back and forth to the consonant, concentrating on keeping your throat calm and open. These consonants can only be sustained for a little while before they become unvoiced. If you try to stay on the double B of "la**bb**ro" too long, it will become a double P! Keep it liquid!

Don't overthink here (or anywhere)! Just experiment with TRULY singing your consonants in the space of the vowel.

32

Today's QR code links to a video of a bassoon teacher teaching a student to articulate with an open throat. He might as well be talking to you! You can also sing your portamento exercises on the sustainable voiced consonants (while... you know what!) Getting comfortable with singing consonants is paramount to your ability to dramatically deliver your text without getting your throat involved.

Not getting your throat involved is paramount to sounding fresh at the end of both Susanna and Butterfly, AND at the end of your career. 'Tis a worthy goal. Just play around with it. Don't take it too seriously. Just enjoy how

ONE BREATH IMPULSE PER PHRASE

means moving through vowel and consonant alike while you maintain the same position of everything except whatever articulator/s must move to produce the consonant.

Move ONLY what MUST move!

Practice Journal

——————— , 20 —

——————— , 20 —

——————— , 20 —

Lezione I
La scala

First Lesson
The Scale

Adagio

Man - ca sol - le - ci - ta Più dell' u - sa - to, An - cor che

s'a - gi - ti Con liɛ - ve fia - to, Fa - ce che pal - pi - ta

Prɛs - so al mo - rir, Fa - ce che pal - pi - ta Prɛs - so al mo - rir.

Many of you may be familiar with the way Vaccai syllabified the first lessons.
We present here the normal syllabification of Italian that you will see in repertoire
so that you can practice your best diction and poetry!

A higher and lower key of each lesson is available at belcantobootcamp.com/vaccai

Lezione I
Salti di terza

First Lesson
Intervals of Thirds

Andantino

Sem - pli - cet - ta tor - to - rɛl - la, Che non ve - de_il suo pe -
ri - glio, Per fug - gir dal cru - do_ar - ti - glio, Vo - la_in grɛm - bo_al cac - cia -
tor. Per fug - gir dal cru - do_ar - ti - glio, Per fug - gir dal cru - do_ar -
ti - glio, Vo - la_in grɛm - bo_al cac - cia - tor, Vo - la_in grɛm - bo_al cac - cia - tor.

Welcome to Lesson 1! Well... Lesson 1 on vowels. Derrick writes about Poetry and Diction in the next chapter before we add text. Note that Lesson 1 comprises both *The Scale* and *Intervals of Thirds*.

For your enjoyment today's QR code links to one of my favorite recordings of legato small intervals – well, all intervals. Just like the singer (and the violinist with one finger on one string – remember him from Two Notes?) the theremin player has to find the next note in relation to the previous.

We sing INTERVALS, not PITCHES.

We prepare ourselves for singing Lesson 1 in perfect Italian by singing Lesson 1 on perfect Italian vowels. Needless to say the first part of Lesson 1 (The Scale) is just a version of our legato tones and semitones from Two Notes. And every interval we will sing after that starts right here as well: with the smooth departure from the first pitch. We will often sing a phrase on one vowel before singing it on the vowels of the poem. Maybe you do that already? Here are some goals to keep in mind:

- The connection between the notes is created by the easy continuation of the breath – not "dragging your voice through all the pitches" as Vaccai will warn us in Lesson 13. We say the portamento is the result of the continuation of the breath, not the goal. Or, put another way:

LEGATO IS THE GOAL, PORTAMENTO IS THE TOOL.

- To achieve the above make sure that you don't "push extra air" at the interval. The air that makes the first pitch is the same air that travels uninterrupted between the pitches and results in the second pitch – and so on. You remember we call it **ONE BREATH IMPULSE PER PHRASE**.
- When you record yourself **the dynamic should be consistent**. No uncontrolled swells on the pitches, no dropping of support before the change of the pitch. Avoid the dreaded 'sausage.' Don't let dynamics happen to you! **Be the boss of your dynamics.** While the voice gets naturally louder when you ascend the scale and naturally softer when you descend (until you enter chest voice, sopranos and mezzos) it is important that we work against this in our practice. No uncontrolled forte in the top. Maintain your support, breath, or whatever your language is coming down the scale. This **equalization of dynamics through the rang**e is one of those skills that is simultaneously basic and advanced.

- Make sure **your vowel stays pure** if you are singing the phrase on one vowel. Make sure you transition from one pure vowel to another smoothly if you sing the phrase on the vowels of the poem.

Now, here is what Derrick has coined "legato culting" some years ago: Spending more time BETWEEN the pitches than ON the pitches! You accepted the religion of legato, but decided to go over there and establish your own cult colony. Don't give portamento a bad name. **Remember:** the purpose of the portamento is to connect gorgeous pitches to each other, not only to sing the stuff between them!

This prompted me to make up a rule: Even in the most cantabile and slow execution of an interval you should **spend no more than 50% of the duration of the pitch moving to the next one.** In repertoire, for example, the first interval of Rodolfo's line "Ta—lor dal mio forziere" in *La bohème*. Don't forget it is a made up rule! It is just to help you stay on the straight and narrow and not "slide around" pointlessly. Splendid singers from the past would happily ignore me and sing as long a portamento as they wish. So should you! But only for expression, not because of sloppy technique.

It is easier to explore this idea in larger intervals where the distance you travel is larger. We will come back to this in Lesson 3 - intervals of sixths.

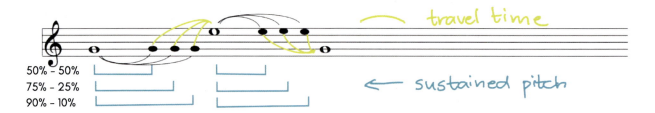

The less time you spend traveling between the pitches the more defined the pitches will sound and the more *marcato* the effect will be. Think for example of Fiordiligi's "Co—me scoglio" and 37 other intervals in that aria. BUT the connection of the breath between the pitches NEVER goes away. Okay, I didn't actually count all the marcato intervals in the aria, but you catch my drift!

Try practicing Lesson 1 in both *cantabile* and *marcato* (and everything in between!) This is where expression lives. If you are new to "old style legato", save *marcato* for another day and stick with *cantabile*.

The examples quoted are not strictly from the bel canto era if you think about the music of Rossini, Donizetti, Bellini and Verdi only. The bel canto style of singing started way earlier and continued through Puccini and Wagner, but sadly not long enough after that... Here we are, fighting for it to reign supreme again!

Practice Journal

——————————— , 20 ——

_____

_____

_____

_____

_____

——————————— , 20 ——

_____

_____

_____

_____

_____

——————————— , 20 ——

_____

_____

_____

_____

_____

Prima le parole, e poi la musica

Since most of the world's singers no longer grow up speaking Italian as a first language, we owe it to ourselves and to the composers and librettists to examine

1. how the language functions: in the operatic libretto we encounter so many archaic Italian words and confusing sentence structures that are not easy to decode – just translating the first poem of Metastasio that Vaccai set is a doozy!
2. how the sound and inherent rhythm of Italian function in relation to musical rhythm – single/double consonants, glides, long/short syllables, for example.

Today we mainly want to focus on the latter. When looking at an Italian poem or a strophe of *versi lirici* (lyric verse: the rhyming verse of equal line length that librettists used for arias and ensembles) that is set to music we have to consider

THREE LEVELS OF 'RHYTHM'

1. **LINGUAL RHYTHM** – every polysyllabic word in Italian has a tonic/-stressed/long syllable. For example: *man*ca sol*le*cita.
    - Let's review Italian syllabification:
        - Double consonants always divide between syllables (sol/le/ci/ta, tor/to/rel/la)
        - **Diphthongs never separate** (lie/ve fia/to) and **this includes final and initial vowels across words!** "Pres/so‿al mo/rir" only has four syllables, because "so" and "al" form only one syllable in the poem. "Che non vede il suo periglio" has eight syllables: che/non/ve/de‿il/suo/pe/ri/glio
        - Sometimes two vowels are adjacent in something called *uno iato* (a hiatus). These do count as two syllables – later we will go into the exact rules, but once you feel comfortable finding poetic meter, these will easily become evident. Examples in Vaccai include "ru/i/na" and "im/pe/tu/o/si" Pronouns like *mio*, *tuo*, and *suo* are technically examples of *iato* but only count as two syllables at the end of a poetic line. The last exception we will discuss here is when you see a diaerisis (commonly called by its German name, *umlaut*) over a vowel (Nemorino sings io/son/sem/pre‿un/i/dï/o/ta to make 8 syllables in the same meter as the other lines of the aria "Quanto è bella, quanto è cara") – the 8 syllables are not made by separating -*pre* and *un*! They go together!
        - L, M, N, R before another consonant go with the preceding vowel: grem/bo, pal/pi/ta
        - S before one or more consonants goes with the following consonant(s): con/tra/sto

○ Let's also review the three basic patterns of word stress in Italian:
- **TRONCO** – the last syllable is tonic/accented/long
  bel/*tà*, mo/*rir*, cac/cia/*tor*
  Parole tronche (truncated words) often have an omitted final vowel or syllable: beltà(de), morir(e), cacciator(e)
- **PIANO** – the next-to-last syllable is long
  pia/no, *man*/ca, u/*sa*/to
- **SDRUCCIOLO** – the second-to-last syllable is long
  sol/*le*/ci/ta, *pal*/pi/ta

2. **POETIC METER** – *Versi lirici*, the rhyming verse of arias and ensembles, is set in strophes of equal line length. **Line length is always counted as if the last word of the poetic line were a piano word.** Let's first examine the second poem of Metastasio that Vaccai sets, excerpted from the opera *Demetrio*.

> Semplicetta tortorella,
> 1 2 3 4 5 6 7 8
> Che non vede il suo periglio,
> 1 2 3 4 5 6 7 8
> Per fuggir dal crudo artiglio
> 1 2 3 4 5 6 7 8
> Vola in grembo al cacciator.
> 1 2 3 4 5 6 7

The first three lines end in piano words (tortor*el*la, pe*ri*glio, ar*ti*glio), and then the last ends, as most final lines do, in a tronco (caccia*tor*). We count 8 syllables in each line – even though the last line only has 7 spoken syllables, it fills the same 'poetic time' to say as if it had 8. The first poem in the Vaccai method has even more variety. If we count syllables, we find

> Manca sollecita (6) *ends in sdrucciolo*
> Più dell'usato, (5) *ends in piano*
> Ancor che s'agiti (6) *ends in sdrucciolo*
> Con lieve fiato (5) *ends in piano*
> Face che palpita (6) *ends in sdrucciolo*
> Presso al morir. (4) *ends in tronco*

Oddio! What do we do here? Well, we know **line length is always determined as if it ended in a piano word**; therefore, we have a 5 syllable poem – a *quinario*. I include a copy from García's *Traité complet de l'art du chant* (1847) outlining where the stresses may fall in different poetic meters. A quinario has primary stress on the fourth syllable. **Try speaking through "Manca sollecita", finding the poetic meter. There is a stress on every line's fourth syllable, but the** secondary poetic stress moves between the first and second syllable. This is what distinguishes poetic meter from lingual rhythm – while words like *man*ca, an*cor*, and *fa*ce certainly have strong syllables, these are not the strongest syllables of the poetic line.

3. MUSICAL NOTATION – We encounter the combination of the particular stresses of words, the flow and rhythm of language, and the simplistic way in which Italian composers notated rhythm. Modern musicians look at older music with the same eyes that have also seen Stravinsky; looking at music of the Baroque, Classical, and Romantic periods requires us to imagine the constraints faced by composers while putting their musical imaginations on paper. Consider the following: **No one Italian word has two equal syllables. How can two truly equal note lengths express a word with two unequal syllables?** We would find the performance of any music without words – piano pieces, chamber music – with no variation of length of note values 'unmusical'. Sophisticated music-making – some call this *"style"* – depends on learning both the unwritten language of music and the notational systems that composers, in order to preserve their works, distilled in ink on a page – decoding which notes 'belong together' within a phrase, where timing is influenced by dissonance and consonance, the interaction of harmonic rhythm (how fast the harmonies change under the the melody), and so on. How much more information we then have as we perform vocal music, combining poetry (*with its own intrinsic meter and rhythm*) and music!

In general, I'd say syllables we want to accent/lengthen come "early" and those we wish to show as unaccented come "late." I definitely, when singing "Manca sollecita," sing the second syllable ("-ca") slightly after the beat. Singing it clearly on the third beat gives it undue accent.

Another aspect to consider is that sometimes downbeats of measures do not correspond to accented syllables in the poem – ideally "Vedrai, carino" or "Regnava nel silenzïo" have no sense of stress on the first downbeat.

The same principle applies in *Manca sollecita* – how can we negate an accent on the downbeat of the first measures in the third and fourth lines of the poem? Especially difficult is having long notes on short syllables of the poem: how do we avoid "aaaaancor che s'agiti cooooooooon lieve fiato"?

How free can we be combining poetry with music? Stretch your imagination. Before you sing your Vaccai exercises, speak through the poetry, making sure you feel a consistent meter and flow. **Support your speech with the same breath energy as your singing!**

ENDECASILLABO correspondant au vers français de 10 syllabes. 6—10 4—8—10 2—4—8—10	« Canto l'armi pietose e il capitano « Che il gran sepolcro liberò di Cristo. » « Levommi il mio pensiero imparte ov' era « Colei ch' io cerco e non ritrovo in terra. »
DECASILLABO correspondant au vers français de 9 syllabes. 4—9 3—6—9	« Voi che sapete che cosa è amor. » « Non più andrai farfallone amoroso. »
NOVENARIO correspondant au vers français de 8 syllabes. 4—8 2—5—8	« A duro stral di ria ventura « Misero me son posto a segno. » « Tormento crudele tiranno « Mi strugge, e mi lacera il core. »
OTTONARIO correspondant au vers français de 7 syllabes. 3—7 3—5—7	«Sovra il sen la man mi posa. » « Casta diva che innargenti. » « Che soave zeffiretto. » « Di piacer mi balza il cor. » « V'e la fresca e limpid' onda « Che il tuo labbro invita a ber
SETTENARIO correspondant au vers français de 6 syllabes. 2—4—6	« Assisa al piè d'un salice. » « Fra poco a me ricovero. »

SENARIO correspondant en français au vers de 5 syllabes. 2—5	« Tornate sereni « Begli astri d'amore « La speme baleni « Nel vostro dolore. »
QUINARIO correspondant au vers français de 4 syllabes. —4	« Voi che sapete « Che cosa è amor. » « Finche han dal vino « Calda la testa. »
QUADRISILLABO correspondant au vers français de 3 syllabes. —3	« Che soave « Zeffiretto « Questa sera « Spirerà. »
TRISILLABO correspondant au vers français de 2 syllabes. —2	« Se cerca « Se dice « L' amico « Dovè « L' amico « Infelice « Rispondi « Mori. »

García, Traité complet de l'art du chant (1847)

Cl.   E m'uccidete intanto.
Egualmente il mio core
Il proprio male ed il rimedio abborre;
E m'affretta il morir chi mi soccorre.
 Manca sollecita
  Più dell'usato,
  Ancor che s'agiti
  Con lieve fiato,
  Face che palpita
  Presso al morir.
 Se consolarmi
  Voi non potete,
  Perchè turbarmi,
  Perchè volete
  La forza accrescere
  Del mio martir? (parte)

Metastasio, Demetrio Act 2, Sc. 13

DEMETRIO

SCENA X.

Barsene.

ERa meglio tacer. Speravo almeno,
Che parlando una volta
Avrebbe la mia fiamma Alceste accolta
Questa piccola speme
Or del tutto è delusa:
Sà la mia fiamma Alceste, e la ricusa.

 Semplicetta tortorella,
  Che non vede il suo periglio,
  Per fuggir dal crudo artiglio
  Vola in grembo al cacciator.
 Voglio anch' io fuggir la pena
  D' un amor fin or tacciuto:
  E m' espongo ad un rifiuto;
  All' oltraggio, ed al rossor. (a)

Metastasio, Demetrio Act 2, Sc. 10

ITALIAN SYLLABIFICATION RULES

POETIC SYLLABIFICATION RULES - THESE APPLY IN LIBRETTI	
Sinalefe is the combination of two vowels across the ending of a word into the start of the next to form **one syllable**. *This is the norm.*	Caro mio ben, 1 2 3 4 credimi almen 1 2 3 4
Sinèresi is the **combination** of the **two syllables of the iato into one** in the **interior** of a poetic line. At the end, they are counted as two.	Caro mio ben, 1 2 3 4 credimi almen 1 2 3 4 Per pietà, bell'idol **mio** 1 2 3 4 5 6 7 8 Non mi dir ch'io sono ingrato 1 2 3 4 5 6 7 8
Dièresi is the **separation** of the **two vowels of a diphthong into two syllables** to conform to the poetic meter. This is shown by a diaeresis (umlaut)	Regnava nel silenzïo 1 2 3 4 5 6 7 8 Io son sempre un idïota 1 2 3 4 5 6 7 8
VOWEL RULES	
WEAK VOWELS (vocali deboli): i, u **STRONG VOWELS** (vocali forti): a, e, o **ACCENTED/STRESSED/TONIC = LONG** both strong and weak vowels can be accented/long, e.g. *cui, mio* are both weak vowels and accented	
A **diphthong** (dittongo) occurs when **two** vowels make "one emission of voice" and therefore constitute **one syllable**. This happens with: **Two non-accented weak vowels: i/u** **or one non-accented weak + one strong vowel: i/u + a/e/o** note that the weak vowel becomes a semi-consonant when combined with the strong vowel	*2 non-accented weak vowels* fiu/mo Giu/sep/pe *1 non-accented weak + 1 strong* lie/ve fia/to fuo/co
A **triphthong** (trittongo) occurs when **three** vowels make "one emission of voice" and therefore constitute **one syllable**. This happens with: **Two weak vowels + one strong vowel**	suoi miei guai
A **hiatus** (uno iato) occurs when **two** vowels make "**two separate emissions of voice**" therefore constitute **two syllables**. This happens with: • **Two strong vowels together** • **an accented weak vowel + another vowel** • after certain prefixes (ri-, re-, bi-, tri-)	*two strong vowels together* so/à/ve pa/ù/ra po/è/ta *accented weak + strong vowel* mì/o *prefixes* ri/al/za/re
CONSONANT RULES	
Letter groups that make one sound are never split.	a/**gn**el/lo la/**sci**a/re vo/**gli**o
Double consonants always divide between syllables	bel/lo tet/to mez/zo
L M N R before another consonant go with the **preceding vowel**	al/to grem/bo pal/pi/ta cor/te/gia/no
S before another consonant goes with the **following consonant**	que/sto con/tra/sto

Practice Journal

_____ , 20 __

_____

_____

_____

_____

_____

_____ , 20 __

_____

_____

_____

_____

_____

_____ , 20 __

list your italian repertoire
and check off when you've
reviewed poetic meter

_____   ○ _____

_____   ○ _____

_____   ○ _____

_____   ○ _____

_____   ○ _____

_____   ○ _____

_____   ○ _____

Lesson 1 on Text

We spent the first part of our journey taking the singer's basic legato skill set apart. How does it all come together? We have to consider

- what we discover and practice when we sing our legato exercises on vowels and consonants,
- think about the rules of poetry and diction, and
- then explore how those things jibe together in an Italian phrase (or any other language for that matter, but for our purposes we now focus on Italian).

We are in the process of making direct connections between "exercise" and "repertoire" - if we don't mindfully connect our technical work to our arias and songs we risk losing out on the fullness of its benefits.

We covered our first two bullet points in the previous two chapters. We applied our daily **One Note** and **Two Notes** work by singing our lesson on vowels first to form the basis of our legato and achieve **ONE BREATH IMPULSE PER PHRASE**. We studied and spoke our poetry and explored *which vowels and consonants are long and short*. This will now become our map for

WHAT GOES WHERE

Here are some basic ground rules for our last bullet point - the jibing together part. **TRAVEL** is our shorthand for what happens between the notes, aka legato.

Reminder: you are not supposed to "drag your voice through the pitches" – travel is how we smoothly sing a line without interrupting the flow of breath.

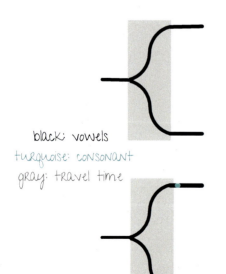

black: vowels
turquoise: consonant
gray: travel time

- If there are *two pitches on one vowel without the interruption of a consonant* you **travel on the vowel** like we did in our legato semitone and tone exercises, e.g. the two pitches on *usato* and *fiato*. Legato ascending and descending intervals, here we go!

- If there is a *single consonant (voiced or unvoiced)*, you **travel on the vowel of the first pitch and the consonant comes quickly once arrived on the second pitch**, e.g. *s'agiti, face.*

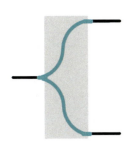

black: vowels
turquoise: consonant
gray: travel time

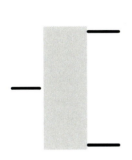

- If there is a double or long sustainable voiced consonant you should travel on that consonant. Remember our exercises on M, N, V, R, L and NG? Traveling on the consonant(s) in these cases ensures the continuation of sound, e.g. "soLLecita" (the LL is long). It is here where our daily practice on **Consonants** is put to good use! (**Reminder**: vowels can be long or short in stressed or unstressed syllables depending on which consonant/s follow them. The A in *manca* is short even though the syllable "man-" is stressed. Another example: *fiamma* – the A is short, the syllable "fiam-" is long, the MM is long).

- If there is *a double unvoiced consonant* the voice still travels from pitch one to pitch two, but **since the travel time is unvoiced we cannot hear the pitch changing**. We either hear
    - the unvoiced sound e.g. *pre<u>ss</u>o* or
    - the pitch changes in silence during the axis of evil – remember P, T and K? e.g. *che<u>pp</u>alpita*. (The P is doubled because of **phrasal doubling** – more about this soon from Derrick)

The correct execution of legato and language supplies answers to two other often encountered problems:

- It helps you not to commit **the mortal sin of doubling an Italian single consonant!** How many times do we hear singers say that they repeatedly receive the note, "Don't double the M in *amore* or the L in *felice*." And they just cannot figure out how to fix it. "I'm not trying to double it!," they cry in despair! Travel on the A in *<u>a</u>more* and the first E in *f<u>e</u>lice* – the vowel before the single consonant. Traveling on the vowel is how you get the following consonant short and single on the new pitch.

- This is also the answer to the question: "**What is the difference between a portamento and a scoop?**" If you travel on the vowel and put the single consonant on the new pitch it is a portamento. If your consonant comes first and THEN you travel on the vowel of the second pitch, you are very much scooping!

I would be so sad if breaking it down like this keeps you from seeing the forest for the trees. I hear singers almost on a daily basis tell me that they are told to work on their legato, but they don't know how. These first chapters have been about helping you improve this essential skill and inspire you ALWAYS to practice these basics. Barre class for singers!

Here is my favorite recording illustrating legato through language – even though in this case it happens to be English. Donald Gramm just about achieves perfection (in my opinion) in Duke's *Luke Havergal*. I must have listened to it a thousand times! Listen to how he sings the voiced consonant cluster on "weste**rn** gate" amongst all the other first rate examples.

He is connecting all the pitches by connecting all the sounds of the language. And by doing so he moves me – every single time I hear it.

In no way does technical perfection leave us cold. I both understand with my brain why it is so good and feel in my soul how the music moves me – the one does not preclude the other. To the contrary: it is the free flowing air that moves me. The sharing without holding back.

Also observe how freely he allows the poetic meter to inform the length of the syllables. No praying at the score by making equal eighth notes here. He is a true disciple of expressing the essence of the score, not reading music like a child.

He understands that the notation is not the music.

Lesson 1 Grammar

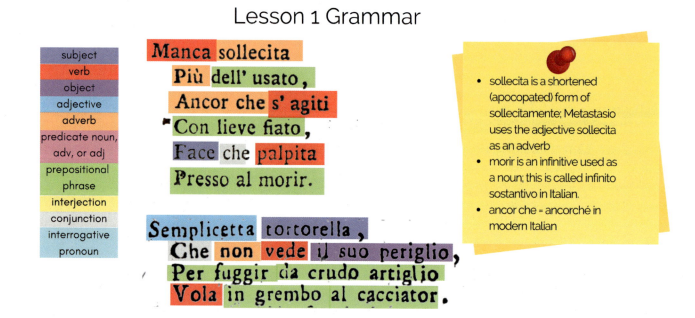

Practice Journal

———————— , 20 —

_____

_____

_____

_____

_____

———————— , 20 —

_____

_____

_____

_____

_____

_____

———————— , 20 —

_____

_____

_____

_____

_____

_____

Where in your repertoire do you sing slow scalar passages? (Good examples include Porgi amor and Dies Bildnis)

_____

_____

_____

_____

_____

_____

Lezione II
Salti di quarta

2nd Lesson
Intervals of Fourths

Adagio

La - scia_il li - do, e il ma - re_in - fi - do A sol -

car tor - na_il noc - chie - ro, E pur sa che men - zo - gne - ro Al - tre

vol - te l'in - gan - nò, Al - tre vol - te l'in - gan - nò, Al - tre

vol - te l'in - gan - nò, Al - tre vol - te l'in - gan - nò.

Lezione II
Salti di quinta

2nd Lesson
Intervals of Fifths

Av - vez - zo_a vi - ve - re Sɛn - za con - for - to,

An - cor nel por - to Pa - vɛn - ti il mar.

Av - vez - zo_a vi - ve - re Sɛn - za con - for - to,

An - cor nel por - to Pa - vɛn - ti il mar.

❋ Singers would have added appoggiaturas or other substitutes for appoggiaturas here in Vaccai's time. You will soon learn how to recognize these places for yourself.

Pre-Shot Routine

As we move forward with our lessons, let us commit to

a) starting our day with Daily Exercises:

- long notes through comfortable range of pitch and dynamic
  (clean onset, sustaining pitch at one dynamic, *messa di voce*)
- two notes connected by portamento
  (all intervals, but especially half steps and whole steps)
- vowels oscillating with consonants

b) practicing our pre-shot routine and staying in the trust mode

Bob Rotella teaches us that the trust mode is the part of your practice where you practice trusting your routine. You cannot wait for the stage or audition room to start trusting your technique.

YOU MUST PRACTICE TRUSTING

Simplify what you think, feel, and/or do before each phrase and do the same thing every time. I'm serious. EVERY TIME. Do NOT judge yourself from phrase to phrase and change your mind about how to sing. Refine your routine and stick to it for a week or more. You can tweak it from time to time. But not every day. And surely not every phrase!

A GOOD PRE-SHOT ROUTINE IS SIMPLE AND REPEATABLE

It should start with
- the target,
- then have something to do with igniting/inspiring/activating your body;
- if it has a third part, it has something to do with helping you follow through and not stop and judge.

Your prompts can be words or just sensations. No long sentences. And it may NOT include the words "don't" or "no". We are ONLY thinking about DO. It only needs to make sense to YOU. Here are some possibilities: **I call it STAYING ON THE POST-IT.**

Sometimes singers who work with me will write their goals/routines on a post-it and send me a picture of it before their auditions or from their dressing rooms before performances. It helps them stay focused on their process and not get distracted by thoughts of fear or doubt.

Lesson 2 includes "Interval of the Fourth" (*Lascia il lido*) and "Interval of the Fifth" (*Avvezzo a vivere*). We will spend a couple chapters here.

Stick to the process we defined for Lesson 1:

- **First, only vowels** to make sure your **one breath impulse per phrase** is intact. Stay smooth in your connections between pitches.
- **Speak the poem,** finding the **poetic meter** (also please make sure that you have your single consonants single and your doubles double).
- **Sing the text,** making sure you **connect the pitches** by connecting the sounds of the language.

These poems are in what verse forms? Revisit Prima le parole e poi la musica for a refresher on versi lirici. Or visit **Italian Training** on **The Gym Floor** on the website.

Today's video is a fun visual accompaniment to the overture of *La gazza ladra* – a great example of an image that can help you stay moving forward in a positive process. One example of visualizing your phrase (continued breath, legato) is a bowling ball moving smoothly down a glistening bowling alley. Our goal is and always remains **one breath impulse per phrase**. Remember that all your thoughts must be about what lies ahead, not what you have done.

what is on your post it?

Janet Hock ▶ Bel Canto Boot Camp
October 5, 2020 ·

During the Rotella book discussions pre-Bootcamp, Rachelle challenged us to think of 3 words as part of the pre-shot routine to be followed before every practice and performance. I have tried this and that, and finally ended up with 3 aspiration words that seem to set things up for me. Plumbline; let-'er-rip; and soar. The plumbline reminds me to straighten my posture (and head) for max lung and resonance spaces. Let-'er-rip came when my voice teacher told me to get more visceral – meaning remember those abdominal muscles – but it also carries a whiff of abandon! Soar came from my study of the alto line in the last movement of Mahler's 2nd Symphony. He moves us from F3 when we all must perish, and ascends up to a glorious G5 that is essential to the harmony in the last bar as we all rise, rise to life! Soar with joy on the breath like hawks cruising the air thermals. Interested to see where others are with their 3 words.

Practice Journal

———————— , 20 —

_____

_____

_____

_____

_____

———————— , 20 —

_____

_____

_____

_____

_____

———————— , 20 —

_____

_____

_____

_____

_____

Let's linger a little longer on Lesson 2. Refer to the previous chapter for your practice inspiration. Revisit Lesson 1 if you have time. All through the course it is useful to go back to earlier lessons to review and refine.

Today we delve a little further into Italian poetry and the libretto of Italian opera. The classic form of the Italian libretto looks like these excerpts from Siface and Demetrio (both Metastasio) – the sources of the poetry of "Lascia il lido" and "Avvezzo a vivere." Vaccai chose to set Metastasio's text for these exercises because setting a champion poet of the Italian language seemed to him a better idea than another set of solfeggio exercises.

Erm. Dunque son nel tuo core
 Onore, fedeltà, costanza, affetto,
 Nomi senza soggetto, idoli vani!
 A' tuoi desiri insani
 Abbandonati, ingrata; il foco mio
 Scordati pur, cangerò stile anch'io.
 Cercherò nuove fiamme,
 Saprò scordarmi anche d'Ismene il nome,
 L'aborrirò quanto l'amai... ma come?
  Lascia il lido,
   E il mare infido
   A solcar torna il nocchiero,
   E pur sa che menzognero
   Altre volte l'ingannò.
  Quel sembiante, — che m'accese,
   Incostante — a me si rese,
   E pur torno a vagheggiarlo.
   E lasciarlo, — oh Dio! non so. *(parte)*

Metastasio, *Siface* Act 2, Sc. 7

ALCESTE.

Sogno? Son desto?
  MITRANE.
    Il primo segno anch'io
Di suddito fedel... (1)
  ALCESTE.
    Mitrane amato,
Non parlarmi per ora.
Lasciami in libertà. Dubito ancora.
  MITRANE.
  Più liete immagini
   Nell'alma aduna;
   Già la Fortuna
   Ti porge il crine:
   È tempo al fine
   Di respirar.
  Avvezzo a vivere
   Senza conforto,
   Ancor nel porto
   Paventi il mar. (2)

(1) In atto d'inginocchiarsi. || (2) Parte.

Metastasio, *Demetrio* Act 3, Sc. 9

It is important to know how to find and recognize authoritative sources for libretti. Check out the QR code for a video guide to finding a trusty libretto.

WHAT AM I SEEING?

- Recitative is left aligned, written in a form called *versi sciolti* (loose/broken verse, similar to blank verse for those who have studied Shakespeare). It typically doesn't rhyme until the last couplet (two lines of poetry) – which concludes the recitative and introduces the coming aria. Sometimes rhyming couplets end particular sections of a longer recitative as well. More on *versi sciolti* later in the course as we prepare the Vaccai recitative lesson, but for now, challenge yourself to count the syllables in each line – even across characters vowels go together – there are either 7 (settenario) or 11 syllables (endecasillabo) in each line of recitative.

- Aria and ensemble are indented from the margin and are written in *versi lirici* (lyric verse) of equal line length and in rhyme. "Lascia il lido" shows, however, a bit of an exception to this rule, in that the first ottonario

  > *Lascia il lido,*
  > *E il mare infido*

  is split across two lines; remember that vowels combine across words to form syllables in Italian.

VERSI LIRICI

Now that we have counted syllables in individual words and lines, we move on to the bigger picture: **poetic meter**. Just like in English and other languages, classical poetry has a consistent pattern of accent or metrical feet.

Versi lirici ('li.ri.tʃi)

- is a rhyming verse of equal line length
- is indented from the left in the libretto, so in the center of the page (you will see more of this as we combine with recitative, which is left-aligned)
- is the verse form for aria and ensemble

Versi lirici looks like this:

> ....
> *la terra e il ciel risponda!*
> *Come la notte i furti miei seconda!*

This is the end of the recitative (versi sciolti)

> Deh, vieni, non tardar, o gioia bella,
> Vieni ove amore per goder t'appella.
> Finché non splende in ciel notturna face
> finché l'aria è ancor bruna e il mondo tace.
> Qui mormora il ruscel, qui scherza l'aura,
> Che col dolce sussurro il cor ristaura;
> Qui ridono i fioretti, e l'erba è fresca:
> Ai piaceri d'amor qui tutto adesca.
> Vieni, ben mio: tra queste piante ascose
> Ti vo' la fronte incoronar di rose.

Deh, vieni, non tardar, o gioia bella,
1   2   3   4   5 6 7 8 9 10 11

Vieni_ove_amore per goder t'appella.
1 2   3   4 5 6   7 8   9 10 11

Finché non splende_in ciel notturna face
1 2   3   4   5   6   7 8 9 10 11

finché l'aria_è_ ancor bruna_ e_ il mondo tace.
1 2 3   4   5   6   7   8 9 10 11

Qui mormora_il ruscel, qui scherza l'aura,
1   2   3   4   5 6   7   8 9   10 11

Che col dolce sussurro_il cor ristaura;
1   2   3 4 5 6   7   8 9 10 11

Qui ridono_i fioretti, e l'erba_è fresca:
1 2 3   4   5 6   7   8   9   10 11

Ai piaceri d'amor qui tutto_adesca.
1 2 3 4 5   6   7 8   9 10 11

Vieni, ben mio: tra queste piante_ascose
1 2   3   4   5   6   7 8   9   10 11

Ti vo' la fronte_incoronar di rose.
1 2   3   4   5   6 7 8 9 10 11

The **endecasillabo** has 11 syllables and is the ultimate Italian meter. You will see every line is the same length in **versi lirici**.

It has an accent:
- always on 10
- sometimes on 4 or 6
- rarely in other places

Deh vieni is an interesting poem: a rare example of an aria that ends in **piano** and not in **tronco**

choose an Italian aria or song and write out the libretto of the versi lirici, count the syllables, and find the verse form

_____
_____
_____
_____
_____
_____
_____
_____
_____
_____
_____
_____
_____
_____
_____
_____

VERSE TYPE *and their typical stresses*	Examples
11 **endecasillabo** 6, **10** 4, (8), **10**	Deh, vieni, non tardar, o gioia bella, 1 2 3 4 5 **6** 7 8 9 **10** 11 Vieni_ove_amore per goder t'appella. 1 2 3 **4** 5 6 7 8 9 **10** 11
10 **decasillabo** 3, 6, **9** 4, **9**	Non so più cosa son, cosa faccio 1 2 **3** 4 5 **6** 7 8 **9** 10 Non più_andrai, farfallone_amoroso 1 2 **3** 4 5 **6** 7 8 **9** 10
8 **ottonario** 3, 5, **7**	Quanto_è bella, quanto_è cara 1 2 **3** 4 5 6 **7** 8 Come Paride vezzoso 1 2 **3** 4 5 6 **7** 8
7 **settenario** 1 or 2, 4, **6**	Tutte le feste_al tempio **1** 2 3 **4** 5 **6** 7 Noi siamo zingarelle 1 **2** 3 **4** 5 **6** 7
6 **senario** 2, **5**	Se_a caso madama Signori, di fuori 1 **2 3** 4 5 6 1 **2 3** 4 **5** 6 la notte ti chiama son già_i suonatori 1 **2** 3 4 **5** 6 1 **2** 3 4 5 6
5 **quinario** 1 or 2, **4**	Se vuol ballare Vedrai, carino 1 2 3 **4** 5 1 **2** 3 **4** 5 signor Contino se sei buonino 1 **2** 3 **4** 5 1 2 3 **4** 5

NOTE: line lengths are counted by where the last accent falls + 1.
  endecasillabo = last accent on **10** plus **1** = **11**
  settenario = last accent on **6** plus **1** = **7**

list all your italian arias and songs and their verse forms

_____

_____

_____

_____

_____

_____

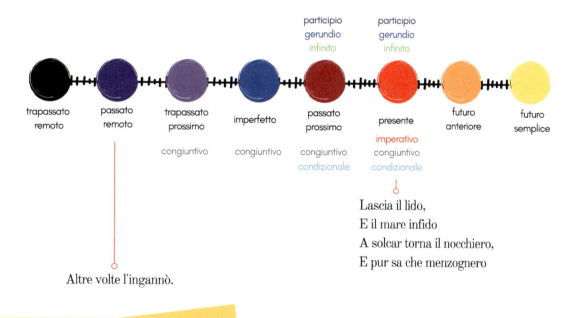

Lesson 2 Grammar

subject	
verb	
object	
adjective	
adverb	
predicate noun, adv, or adj	
prepositional phrase	
interjection	
conjunction	
interrogative pronoun	

Lascia il lido,
E il mare infido
A solcar torna il nocchiero,
E pur sa che menzognero
Altre volte l'ingannò.

Avvezzo a vivere
Senza conforto,
Ancor nel porto
Paventi il mar.

participio gerundio infinito

participio gerundio infinito

trapassato remoto	passato remoto	trapassato prossimo	imperfetto	passato prossimo	presente	futuro anteriore	futuro semplice
		congiuntivo	congiuntivo	congiuntivo condizionale	imperativo congiuntivo condizionale		

Lascia il lido,
E il mare infido
A solcar torna il nocchiero,
E pur sa che menzognero

Altre volte l'ingannò.

- In some editions of Vaccai he writes "pavento il mar" - "I fear the sea"; however, in the original opera of Metastasio it is in the second person - "you fear the sea" - paventi.

Avvezzo a vivere
Senza conforto,
Ancor nel porto
Paventi il mar.

Refer to the following page for a full diagram on verb tenses and moods.

VERB TENSES AND MOODS

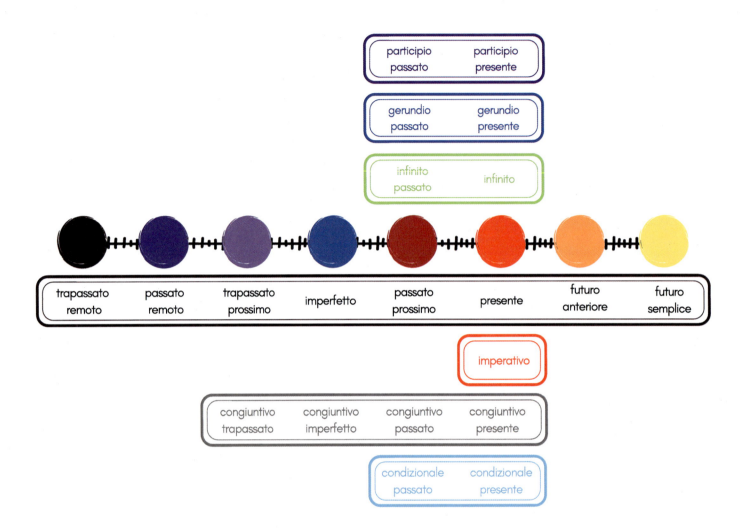

Tenses indicate time.
Past? Present? Future?
Compound tenses show the relationship
of one action to another.

indicativo **imperativo** **congiuntivo** **condizionale**
You are singing. **Sing!** If you were to sing... You would sing.

Finite moods indicate degree of obligation, possibility,
conditionality, probability. Statement, command, wish?

infinito gerundio participio
Infinite moods do not define person, number, or time.

Practice Journal

—————————— , 20 —

_____
_____
_____
_____
_____
_____

—————————— , 20 —

_____
_____
_____
_____
_____

—————————— , 20 —

_____
_____
_____
_____
_____

Lezione III
Salti di sesta

3rd Lesson
Intervals of Sixths

Andantino

Bɛl - la pro - va‿è d'al - ma for - te L'ɛs - ser pla - ci - da‿e se -

re - na Nel sof - frir l'in - giu - sta pe - na D'u - na col - pa che non

ha. Bɛl - la pro - va‿è d'al - ma for - te L'ɛs - ser pla - ci - da‿e se -

re - na Nel sof - frir l'in - giu - sta pe - na D'u - na col - pa che non ha.

Welcome to Lesson 3 which has only one vocalise on the interval of the sixth, *Bella prova è d'alma forte.* Today we explore another mantra:

WE SING INTERVALS, NOT PITCHES

When the intervals get bigger in Vaccai, it presents a good opportunity to practice *traveling between the pitches at different tempos.* Of course you can (and should) practice this in ALL your intervals, but, especially for less advanced singers, it is easier to refine speed of portamento in the bigger ones.

Remember we made up that rule that 50% is the cut off point beyond which you are "legato culting"? If you practice the 1:1 relationship between *pitch* and *travel*, you are investing practice time in your most cantabile expression. The more time you spend on the pitches and the faster you travel between them, the more *marcato* your delivery. How good can you get at this? Can you do 2:1? 3:1? 4:1? And all the relationships in between? Can you get to the place where the travel time is SO fast that only you (and I!) would know it is there? The better you get at managing "travel time", the more possibilities of expression you will have at your disposal.

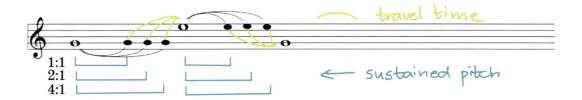

Remember that **one breath impulse per phrase** remains your goal. Don't shove your breath at the interval! The breath on which you travel is the same breath you initiated in your onset. THIS is why refining your onsets is so important. Make sure your portamento is smooth (no stopping on any intermediate pitches), dynamically blended with the rest of the phrase and with consistent spin (vibrato). Failing to do so means you've lost the legato you were striving for in the first place.

Why not try to play with this idea while singing Lesson 3 on vowels only? You should also spend time speaking the poem (on the voice and legato of course). Tomorrow is another day – you can put them together then!

You may have heard, "there is no portamento in Mozart," "there is no portamento in Wagner," or "there is no portamento in French song." A short visit to historic singers on YouTube will disprove these hypotheses. Singers like Lilli Lehmann and Ninon Vallin would roll their eyes at these modern urban legends. When confronted with this opinion in a professional setting, you will find being able to adjust your **travel time** quite useful

Listen to these masters moving the air between pitches through all the different sounds in all the different languages. Can you hear how varied the relationships between *pitch* and *travel* are? Listen both to HOW they sing and WHAT they sing – you can understand their technical efficiency and be touched by them at the same time.

TECHNIQUE IS THE VEHICLE OF EXPRESSION

If you are new to listening to early recordings, especially the pre-microphone ones, this video by Bel Canto Sunday Matinée host Steven Tharp is a great crash course in training your ears. During this course we will often listen to recordings made in the early days of recording history. We hope to inspire you to delve deep into the history of recorded sound. Most all of it is available on YouTube these days!

Practice Journal _____ , 20 ___

_____ , 20 ___

_____ , 20 ___

Let him learn the Manner to glide with the Vowels, and to drag the Voice gently from the high to the lower Notes, which, thro' Qualifications necessary for singing well, cannot possibly be learn'd from Sol-fa-ing only, and are overlooked by the Unskilful.   Tosi: *Observations on the Florid Song*, 1723

By this portamento is meant nothing but a passing, tying the voice, from one note to the next with perfect proportion and union, as much in ascending as descending. It will then become more and more beautiful and perfected the less it is interrupted by taking breath, because it ought to be a just and limpid gradation, which should be maintained and tied in the passage from one note to another. The portamento cannot be acquired by any scholar who has not already united the two registers, which are in everyone separated.   Mancini: *Practical Reflections on Figured Singing*, 1774

Through some disjunct intervals [the singer] will carry the voice with such an inflection that it will pass by way of an indefinite number of sounds of which one cannot specify the pitch.
        Asioli: *Scale e salti per il solfeggio, Preparazione al canto ed ariette*, 1814

By carrying the voice from one note to another, it is not meant that you should drag or drawl the voice through all the intermediate intervals, an abuse that is frequently committed - but it means to "unite" perfectly the one note with the other.   Vaccai: M*etodo Pratico di Canto Italiano per Camera*, 1833

Carrying the voice (*port de voix - portamento di voce*) is leading from one pitch to another passing through all the intermediary pitches possible. The portamento can include everything from the semitone to the biggest range of the voice. Its length is taken on the last portion of the note that is left. The speed depends on the character of the music to which it belongs.

Connecting pitches (*vocalisation liée - agilità legata e granita*) is passing from one pitch to the other in a clean, subtle, spontaneous way, without letting the voice be interrupted or tarry on an intermediate pitch...So that legato coloratura shows all the characteristics of perfection, it is necessary that the intonation be irreproachably just; it is necessary that all the notes have an equality of value, sound, and color, and finally that all the pitches be equally legato. We can hardly achieve this goal after a year and a half of study.

        García: *A Complete Treatise on the Art of Singing* Part I, 1847

Without legato there is no singing; and, the two things that render the human voice superior to every other instrument are the power of legato, and the variation in color.
        F. Lamperti: *The Art of Singing According to Ancient Tradition and Personal Experience*, 1884

The pupil must observe a strict legato, a smooth and unbroken passage from one tone to the other. The breath must not be interrupted between the tones, but flow evenly as if a single tone were sung.
        G.B. Lamperti: *The Technics of Bel Canto*, 1905

Legato was often taught by first rehearsing deliberate, audible, portamenti between pitches, which were subsequently reduced in duration to the point of imperceptability. Voice in this regard is analogous to a string instrument on which pitch is changed with the tuning key, not on the fingerboard, and for which the bow continues while the string is being retuned. It involves very rapid changes in vocal fold tension from one sustained, vibrant pitch, to the next, rapidly moving through the intervening micro-pitches too quickly for them to be perceived.   Kenneth Bozeman: *Kinesthetic Voice Pedagogy 2*, 2021

Making Music

The challenge for today is to make music!

Time to put words to music in Lesson 3. Keep going back to the previous lessons as well – maybe you are doing that already. Good job! Allow your dramatic and musical imagination to guide your voice. Remember that the ultimate goal is not perfection – such a goal is unattainable. The goal is to improve your skills so that you can execute what is in your imagination. Show me how you think the music goes. Is your voice doing what you ask it to do?

What is your favorite aria or song? Challenge yourself to use the provided spaces to write down specific places in your repertoire where Vaccai can help you. Recognizing the required skill set in your music is paramount if you are going to own it. Expression without working around technical deficiencies is the goal.

My favorite "aria of sixths" is **Cinta di fiori** from *I puritani*. What a gorgeous piece! And how devastatingly beautiful it is when executed in legato without the dreaded "H's"! Lesson 3 will help you get there.

Today's listening is a compilation of different singers singing this aria. Purpose here is not to judge the singer, but to train your ear. When are they successful, and when are they less so? What are you listening to, and what are you learning from listening? All hail Bellini – what a tune!

What repertoire do you sing that regularly features or repeats certain wider intervals? Keep them legato!

_____

_____

_____

_____

_____

Lesson 3 Grammar

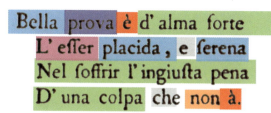

Bella **prova** è d' alma forte
L' esser placida, e serena
Nel soffrir l'ingiusta pena
D' una colpa che **non** à.

Are you learning to recognize old forms of script and antiquated spellings?
*For example, **serena** is serena and **à** is ha in modern Italian.*

Practice Journal

——————————— , 20 —

_____

_____

_____

_____

——————————— , 20 —

_____

_____

_____

_____

——————————— , 20 —

_____

_____

_____

_____

Lezione IV

Salti di settima

4th Lesson

Intervals of Sevenths

Welcome to *Salti di settima – Intervals of Sevenths*. We'll get to octaves in a couple of chapters.

Lesson 4 is a first rate exercise of **chest/head transition** – especially for sopranos and mezzo-sopranos. The music of Fiordiligi, Rosina, Cenerentola, and all their friends becomes a nightmare if this skill has not been sufficiently trained. No amount of prayer can get you through the alto solos in *Messiah* without facility in singing across the registers. You either get stuck in head voice or you get stuck in chest voice and you throw your hands in the air screaming, "WHY?! WHY DID YOU WRITE IT THIS WAY?!" Many a Susanna gets herself stuck in head voice in *Deh vieni non tardar* and wonders where her chest voice has gone … poverina!

The "up to F4 in chest" of Viardot and others (as we explored in the first part of our journey) had a profound effect on all composers who wrote for singers trained in the bel canto tradition – not only Rossini, Donizetti, Bellini and Verdi. Mozart and Wagner take their places in the lineup with pride. **Reminder:** We are exploring here the *bel canto style of singing* – not merely the compositional style. It is hard to know if composers consciously or subconsciously explored laryngeal registration in their compositions. Remember that composers wrote (and still do write) for the singers of their time. Even a cursory glance at the treatises of their time reveals how consistently the blending of the registration shift around F4 was taught, as we have seen multiple times already.

This is why we find F4 and E♭4 as the "bottom pitches" in Leonora's cabaletta *Di tale amor*, Violetta's *Sempre libera*, Amina's *Ah non giunge*. Where do you find these pitches in your repertoire? Jot them down in your Practice Journal or Repertoire Application box. Listen to Leontyne Price and Rosina Storchio for example if you don't believe me. The earlier the recording you find, the better the chance that the F's and E-flats are in chest. It almost functions like string crossings in the violin. Your chest voice as your G string! Or as Derrick says, "A soprano without a chest voice is like a pianist without a left pinky!"

I would go even further. Even though the pitches up to F4 make up a relatively small percentage of pitches in a treble aria/song/operatic role, I fully experience a voice as "half a voice" when chest-dominant singing is absent. For me the chest voice completes the voice. It reveals the complete soul of the character. The converse is true for the non-treble voice: The absence of head voice leaves me unfulfilled. Where is the "sweet part" of the voice? For me the perfect human voice must exhibit both the *animus* and the *anima*.

The laryngeal registers are in a constant dance with each other.
They complement each other.
Sometimes one leads. Sometimes the other.
They move together seamlessly as a couple.

It is NOT TRUE that composers knew that the treble voice is weak at the bottom. They knew quite the opposite. On the other hand, please note that nobody ever told you to sing every chest-dominant note as loudly as you possibly can. Composers expect you to have control of your transition and have options of dynamics in both chest and head voice. You can do this!

Much has been written on this topic and sometimes people are not on the same page about what is fact and what is opinion. My thoughts here are based both on what I believe to be fact and my practical experience as a bel canto coach.

There are two biological (laryngeal) registers – most people call them chest voice and head voice. The geeks among us use the terms *thyroarytenoid dominance* and *cricothyroid dominance*, or *Mode 1* and *Mode 2*. (Refer to our table in the *Messa di voce* chapter in **Daily Exercises**. It is pretty easy to hear the difference - you can even see it on the spectrogram in Voce Vista (example on the next page). I often ask my young students to listen to pop music to train their ears. I prefer Joni Mitchell, but you do you. Can you tell when they are singing chest-dominant or head-dominant?

Blending of the registers means being able to move smoothly between the two biological registers, NOT creating a third one. Review both *Messa di voce* and *Laryngeal Registration* in **Advanced Daily Exercises** if you are confused about the term "mix." I suggest you just banish the word from your vocabulary – it is not useful. Every classically produced tone is "mixed." Attaching this word to some notes and not others is just confusing.

You cannot blend two things if you don't know what they are!
Let's take some practical steps to clarify them.

Don't be so afraid! Nobody will die if we can hear the transition! In today's listening you will be able to hear the laryngeal transitions if you listen closely - and these are some of the best singers you can listen to! Call it "the speaking register" if chest scares you. It is as good a description as any. "Walking back and forth around the laryngeal passaggio" is just the natural thing to do.

The trick is not to associate chest voice only with singing loudly.

Exercises that really DO pull attention to the registration switches are a good way to define the two things you are "mixing" on a day to day basis. And some repertoire is written to show off laryngeal registration in an obvious way. If you refine this skill, you will never have to say, "Oh, I've been singing so much high stuff that now I cannot find my lower voice in *Deh vieni non tardar*."

If you know where your chest voice is, you cannot lose it!

auditory roughness

This is a spectrogram representing a soprano switching between head-dominant /u/ on E♭4 and chest-dominant /a/ on the same pitch with the goal of the same dynamic. Scan the QR code to listen.

What you see is an increase in **auditory roughness** when she is in chest voice – partials close to each other are boosted.

Practice *Salti di settima* on vowels only (or even on a consonant like /m/) and see if you can build towards singing everything up to F4 in LIGHT chest. Do NOT press the issue. If, at this stage, you are only able to sing in a calm, not pressed chest voice up to C4 or so... fine! You have time! Consider singing the exercise in a lower key so you can practice the low notes calmly in chest. You can find the lower key at belcantobootcamp.com/vaccai. It has been picked specifically to practice classic laryngeal registration. Embrace the thought of

CALM, NOT PRESSED CHEST VOICE IN MEDIUM TO SOFT DYNAMIC

Some of my singers find it easiest to sing the chest-dominant pitches on /i/ and the head-dominant pitches on /u/ to get the laryngeal tilt going. If your /i/ tends to get your jaw involved let's use /a/ instead. Experiment to see what works for you. I also have a singer who finds her calmest chest voice on /u/! Makes no sense to me, but there you have it!

Do you have control of your registration? Can you enter chest in a dynamic of your choice? Or are you going *splat!* in there? Are you avoiding the issue altogether by staying in head voice, which sounds weak compared to the rest of the phrase no matter how hard you try? Which other arias or songs would benefit from smooth chest/head transition? Writing them down will help you focus your attention, we promise!

WHERE CAN MY REGISTRATION IMPROVE?

_____

_____

_____

_____

_____

_____

Come YODEL with me! seems to be fun for singers I work with and you must be willing to have fun if you are going to grow. The exercise has the same purpose as the classic ones like Viardot: to exercise chest voice up to F4, while also training head voice down to C4. Viardot (like most of the bel canto instructors) treats F4 as the laryngeal passaggio – this was not a question of opinion. Nor was it proclaimed that "all voices are different."

All voices ARE different, but there is not a different "technique" for every voice.

As we have seen elsewhere the old treatises do not distinguish between treble and non-treble voices when it comes to the F4 laryngeal passaggio. The human voice moves from chest to head dominance naturally in the vicinity of this pitch and bel canto training teaches the professional singer to achieve this smoothly and elegantly.

In performance **the treble voice** should rarely sing in head voice dominance (Mode 2) below E or E ♭, but it is useful to exercise it to inform softer dynamics in chest dominance on these pitches. Just like practicing in falsetto aids the dynamic options of the non-treble voice in chest above E ♭. The human voice is a continuum and the treble and non-treble voice mirror each other.

Sopranos and mezzos have to traverse this pivot point ALL THE TIME, and the old divas did so masterfully – we are beyond excited when we discover a new diva who does so with grace and ease!

Non-treble voices sang in public with more head voice above this passaggio. Remember that the "do di petto" (chest voice on C5) marked a departure from this when in 1837 Gilbert Duprez rolled it out in Paris during Rossini's magnificent Guillaume Tell. In no way did this usher in "all-chest-all-the-time" yet. That came later.

While tenors and baritones/basses in the modern world sing in chest-dominant production only, laryngeal registration exercises ("flipping between chest and falsetto") builds dynamic possibilities below, through, and above the passaggio – remember that dynamics are a result of registration.

To sing louder, a singer adds 'threads' of chest to the mix of any note – whether it is chest-dominant or not.
To sing softer, a singer adds 'threads' of head to the mix of any note – whether head-dominant or not.

You can find more registration exercises in the Registration Circuit on The Gym Floor. We'll get to all of them during this course, though, so don't rush it!

Today's QR code takes you to *Listen to Registration*.

Be inspired! Happy yodeling!

Sing whatever is your easiest chest vowel on the bottom (i or a)

[c. h. c. h. c. h. c. h. h.]

[c. chest
h. head]

If you are nervous before your
Met debut sing the words below!

i u i u i u i u u

High on a hill was a lonely goat-herd   Lay ee odle lay ee odl lay hee hoo

Sing also in F# (starting on C#)
G (starting on D)
Ab (starting on Eb)
A (starting on E)
Bb (starting on F)

Then giggle and shake
off the nervous because
you know how to do this!

BUT only as high as you can sing the lowest note in chest easily —
NO BELTING!

Sing also in E (starting on B)
Eb (starting on Bb)
D (starting on A)
C# (starting on G#)
C (starting on G)

AND keep the upper notes in head easily. Middle C and C# will not
be loud in head voice, but it essential to build for good register
transitions. **NO PUSHING!**

Practice Journal   _____, 20__

_____

_____

_____

_____

COME YODEL WITH ME - TENOR

The purpose of this practice sheet is to develop head voice coordination, aka letting your falsetto inform your chest dominant singing past the passaggio.

DYNAMICS are EVERYTHING!

[c. chest f. falsetto]

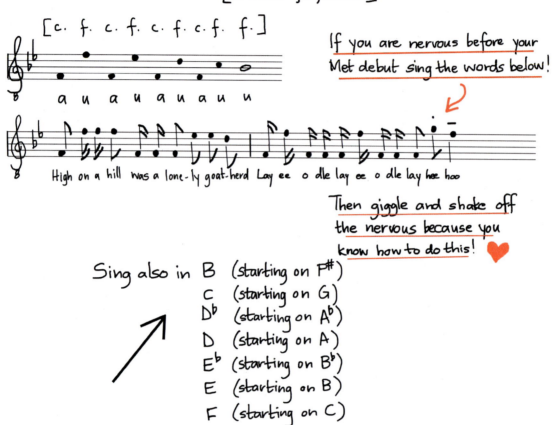

[c. f. c. f. c. f. c. f. f.]

a u a u a u a u u

If you are nervous before your Met debut sing the words below!

High on a hill was a lone-ly goat-herd Lay ee o dle lay ee o dle lay hee hoo

Then giggle and shake off the nervous because you know how to do this!

Sing also in B (starting on F#)
C (starting on G)
D♭ (starting on A♭)
D (starting on A)
E♭ (starting on B♭)
E (starting on B)
F (starting on C)

BUT only as high as you can sing the highest falsetto note EASILY!

NO REINFORCING THE FALSETTO!

YOU ARE NOT A COUNTER TENOR!

Practice Journal

_____ , 20___

_____

_____

_____

_____

The purpose of this practice sheet is to develop head voice coordination, aka letting your falsetto inform your chest dominant singing past the passaggio.

DYNAMICS are EVERYTHING! ❤️

[c. chest   f. falsetto]

[c. f. c. f. c. f. c. f. f.]

a u a u a u a u u

If you are nervous before your Met debut sing the words below!

High on a hill was a lone-ly goat-herd Lay ee o dle lay ee o dle lay hee hoo

Then giggle and shake off the nervous because you know how to do this! ❤️

Sing also in A (starting on E)
              B♭ (starting on F)
              B (starting on F♯)
              C (starting on G)
              D♭ (starting on A♭)
              D (starting on A)
              E♭ (starting on B♭)

BUT only as high as you can sing the highest falsetto note **EASILY!**

❤️ **NO REINFORCING THE FALSETTO!** ❤️
YOU ARE NOT A COUNTER TENOR!

Practice Journal

_____ , 20__

_____
_____
_____
_____
_____

Phrasal Doubling and Assimilation

Today we explore the concept of **phrasal doubling** or *raddoppiamento fonosintattico*. This phenomenon occurs in the Italian language chiefly as a homage to its Latin roots, or as the kids say nowadays, "we got the receipts." As Latin morphed into Italian, we see both that spelling changed AND that there was a lasting effect on pronunciation. Many of the double consonants that we see spelled out are the evolution/assimilation of consonant clusters from Latin:

octo /kt/ → otto   saxum /ks/ → sasso   somno /mn/ → sonno

In Italian there are four sounds that **auto-double** when between vowels:

sc (lasciare)   gn (regno)   gl (figlio)
z/zz (azione [unvoiced /ts/], mezzo [voiced /dz/])

And these are "receipts" from Latin, for example:

lasciare /ʃːʃ/ is from Latin laxare /ks/
azione /tːts/ <L actus /kt/
olezzo /dːdz/ <L olidus /d/

> words that include unvoiced z /ts/ in Italian usually come from Latin words with T + vowel; voiced z /dz/ usually comes from Latin D + vowel
> prezzo /prɛtːtso/ <L pretius
> pranzo /prandzo/ <L prandium

The same influence from Latin is what causes the phenomenon of phrasal doubling – where there were more consonant sounds between words in Latin, the Italians preserved this effect by doubling the initial consonant after certain words, falling into the groups of

Words that cause doubling after

All monosyllabic words with written accents such as

| già | *già tanto* → /dʒatːtanto/ |
| è | *è vero* → /ɛvːvero/ |

Strong/tonic (monosyllabic) words such as

a	*a voi* → /avːvoi/
che	*che dici* → /kedːditʃi/
tu	*tu sei* → /tusːsɛi/

All polysyllabic words with stress on the final syllable such as

città	*città grande* → /tʃitːtagːgrande/
sarà	*sarà forse* → /sarafːforse/
perché	*perché chiusa* → /perkekːkjuza/

Five piano words

come	*come Paride* → /komepːparide/
dove/ove	*dove sei* → /dovesːsɛi/
qualche	
sopra/sovra	
contra	(not contro)

> Latin: a**d** vos
> Italian: a**vv**oi
>
> Archaic Italian:
> citta**de** grande
> Modern Italian:
> città**gg**rande

Words that cause doubling before

Religious references (Dio, dei, dei, dea)

Dio *o Dio* → /o**d:d**io/

dei *o dei* → /o**d:d**ɛi/

Certain fixed names, again religious (Maria)

Maria *Ave Maria* → /ave**m:m**aria/

Over time, Italian incorporated these phrasal doublings in spelling – as with any development, it is far from consistent, but sometimes combinations like

a presto	are written	a**pp**resto
a bastanza		a**bb**astanza
da vero		da**vv**ero
da che		da**cc**hé
è vero		e**vv**ero
lo saprò		sapro**ll**o (saprò lo, future tense)
mi mancò		manco**mm**i (mancò mi, passato remoto)

Pronunciation of other consonants in Italian are influenced by **assimilation.** We see this automatically reflected in words like

i**n**- (not) + **m**obile → i**mm**obile

Gia**n** + **B**attista → Gia**mb**attista

where **N** changes to **M** because of the following consonant – to make the pronunciation more fluid. We must also recognize these **assimilation patterns** when they are not written, but still honored in pronunciation; they neutralize the position of the nasal consonant and move it closer to the position of the following sound.

N before B and P → M

un bacio → /u**m**batʃo/

in petto → /i**m**pɛt:to/

N before V and F → what we call a "Chipmunk M"

invece → /i**ɱ**vetʃe/

conforto → /co**ɱ**fɔrto/

N before C and G → NG

ancora → /a**ŋ**kora/

ingrato → /i**ŋ**grato/

This is an instructive video on the history of the Italian language, different Italian accents, and the concept of a developed "standard Italian" that was really invented in the twentieth century. This "dizione" is used for acting and film dubbing, as well as the "standard Italian" we sing. You can put the closed captions to English or one of a few other languages if you desire. The presenter of Podcast Italiano also has a video specifically on phrasal doubling, only in Italian.

Phrasal Doubling Cheat Sheet

Vaccai Texts

THESE CAUSE FIRST CONSONANT OF NEXT WORD TO DOUBLE	
STRONG MONOSYLLABLES/MONOSYLLABLES WITH WRITTEN ACCENT	
Prepositions	a da tra fra su
Pronouns	tu me˙ te˙ sé chi che ciò
Adverbs	qui qua lì là giù già più sì
Adjective	blu
Number	tre
Answer Words	sì no
Nouns	tè gru re
Shortened nouns	ca'(sa) fé(de) fra(te)
	mo'(do) pre'(te) piè(de)
Verbs	è ho ha do dà di'
	fa fu sa sto sta va
Conjunctions	se ma o e né
Note Names	do re mi fa sol la si
Letter Names	a bi/be ci/ce di/de
Greek Letters	e gi/ge i ca pi/pe
	qu/cu ti/te u vu/vi
	mi chi ni xi pi rho phi psi
	˙only when tonic/strong (a me piace ✔, me lo dico ✘)
POLYSYLLABLES WITH ACCENTED FINAL SYLLABLE (TRONCO)	
Tronco nouns like	caffè
Nouns that lost a syllable	beltà(de) città(de) virtù(de)
Conjunctions like	perché poiché però cosi
Verb forms like	sarà vedrà parti parlerò
SYLLABLES WITH ACCENTED NEXT-TO-LAST SYLLABLE (PIANO)	
Five prepositions	come contra dove/ove
	sopra/sovra qualche
FIRST CONSONANT OF THESE WORDS DOUBLES AFTER VOWEL	
Religious References	Dio dea dee dei
Certain Fixed Expressions	Ave Maria Spirito Santo
THESE WORDS DO NOT CAUSE DOUBLING	
Unstressed Pronouns	me te se ce ve ne
	mi ti si ci vi gli
Articles like	lo la li i gli
Preposition	di

Maŋca sollecita
Piùddell'usato,
Aŋcor chess'agiti
Con liɛve fiato
Face cheppalpita
Prɛsso al morir.

Semplicetta tortorɛlla
Chennoŋ vede il suo periglio,
Per fuggir dal crudo artiglio
Vola iŋ grɛmbo al cacciator.
gl = /ʎːʎ/

Lascia il lido e il mare imɲfido
assolcar torna il nocchiɛro
eppur sacchemmenzogngnɛro
altre volte l'iŋganno.
sc = /ʃːʃ/ **gn** = /ɲːɲ/

Avvezzo avvivere
Senza comɱforto
Aŋcor nel porto
Paventi il mar.

Bella prova ɛdd'alma forte
L'ɛsser placida esserena
Nel soffrir l'ingiusta pena
D'una colpa chennon ha.

Frall'ombre un lampo solo
Basta al nocchiɛr sagace
Cheggiàrritrova il polo
Cherriconosce il mar.
sc = /ʃːʃ/

Lesson 4 Grammar

subject	
verb	
object	
adjective	
adverb	
predicate noun, adv, or adj	

Fra l'ombre un lampo solo
Basta al nocchier sagace
Che già ritrova il polo,
Già riconosce il mar.

prepositional phrase	
interjection	
conjunction	
interrogative	
pronoun	

Practice Journal

——————— , 20 —

_____

_____

_____

_____

_____

_____

——————— , 20 —

_____

_____

_____

_____

——————— , 20 —

_____

_____

_____

_____

_____

_____

Where do you need to remember phrasal doubling in your repertoire?

_____

_____

_____

_____

_____

_____

Lezione IV
Salti di ottava

4th Lesson
Intervals of Octaves

This is our only chapter on the second part of Lesson 4 – *Salti di ottava (Intervals of Octaves)*. In *Quell'onda che ruina,* you can review many topics we have discussed.

Poetic Meter

Quell'onda che ruïna *(settenario piano)*
Balza, si frange e mormora *(settenario sdrucciolo)*
Ma limpida si fa. *(settenario tronco)*

When you count the syllables of the poetic lines you will arrive at seven, eight, and six, respectively. Since the second line ends in a sdrucciolo (**mor**mora) and the third line ends in a tronco (**fa**), these lines all count poetically as seven syllable lines *(settenari)*. Another way to explain this is that all these lines take the same amount of poetic time as a s*ettenario piano*.

> **Reminder:** ru/i/na is an example of **iato** – like paura and other words where an i or u is stressed and combined with another vowel.

Think about how the line length influences the composer's choices; for example, you'll see the stressed syllables here align with the downbeats, despite how many unaccented syllables follow. This topic is going to come up in an interesting way when we discuss the appoggiatura in detail.

Legato through Consonants

Keep your breath moving smoothly through the consonants in the big intervals. These big intervals really clarify what is going on from a pitch and consonant perspective *between the notes*, or as we call it, **TRAVEL TIME .** This is where we create our true legato line. Remember to stay in control of your dynamics. No sausages! Revisit *Lesson 1 on Text* if you need a refresher.

Registration for Treble Voices

This vocalise offers the treble voice another fantastic opportunity to practice smooth chest/head transitions. Until the final line it invites you to alternate clearly and efficiently between the two laryngeal registers. The final line affords you the opportunity to see how smoothly you can do it in a scale. Can you transition smoothly at different places in this scale? Re-visit the BCBC five note descending scale exercise in **BCBC Switch Exercises** in *Daily Exercises: Laryngeal Registration.*

Legato in Small Intervals

Remember our legato tone and semitone exercises from **Two Notes**? Are you still doing them? Make sure that you don't end up with those pesky H's in *ru/i/na* and *lim/pi/da* (in the final scalre). If you have stepped away from your onset, *messa di voce* and portamento exercises, you are not starting your days with the basics of barre class. You must.

Hermann Klein was an English voice teacher who became the first chairman of the National Association of Teachers of Singing while he lived in New York between 1901 and 1909. In his capacity as musical advisor to Columbia Records he developed his *Phono-Vocal Method of Learning Singing with the Aid of a Gramophone*. A lot can be learned from listening to these lessons.

Janet Spencer (the contralto in the QR code) studied with Hermann Klein, who studied with Garcìa, who himself was a contemporary of Vaccai. In the same way, many early recordings can be traced back to singers, teachers, or composers from a generation or two before the advent of sound reproduction. Let me make a comment here in case we have in our midst those who believe one cannot deduce anything from lineage because

- singers do not necessarily sound like their teachers and
- the true genius student advances the world by "breaking the rules" they are taught.

When it comes to singing, I don't believe this to be a useful argument because

- even though each voice has a unique sound, we can absolutely hear how someone was taught if we know what we are listening for, and
- we are trying to learn something about how people used to sing before "the rules" started to be broken – wittingly or unwittingly. The microphone is maybe the biggest "culprit" here – the singer who must sing un-amplified over an orchestra in a large space cannot afford to break that many rules. "The rules" are intricately linked to the audibility of the unamplified voice. For an in-depth discussion about the influence of the microphone with BCBC's favorite guest lecturer, Will Crutchfield, scan the QR code below.

When we listen to early recordings it is evident that there were rules and that they were followed pretty consistently for quite a long time. They often seem to be accurate depictions of the methods of singing described in words (treatises) long before it was possible to reproduce sound. We read in these treatises what the rules were; we hear in the earliest recordings that singers followed them. Whether you choose to follow them yourself will

be up to you. At which point beyond the extended bel canto repertoire do you decide that the bel canto principles curtail either the composer's intent or your desired expression of what you know/believe their intent to be? Often I hear from professional singers: "The better I sing my bel canto, the better I sing my contemporary repertoire."

Steven Tharp's **Bel Canto Sunday Matinées** explore early recordings and celebrate extraordinary singers you might know but, even better, introduce you to a multitude I suspect you might not. He introduces me to new ones all the time! You can find these sessions archived in the Members Area on our website. Find his list of "Singers You Should Know" on p. 95.

Lesson 4 Grammar cont'd

subject
verb
object
adjective
adverb
predicate noun, adv, or adj
prepositional phrase
interjection
conjunction
interrogative pronoun

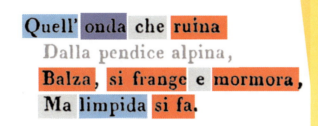

Quell' onda che ruina
Dalla pendice alpina,
Balza, si frange e mormora,
Ma limpida si fa.

ruina is from an antiquated form, **ruinare**, of **rovinare**

Vaccai omitted one line of the quatrain

Practice Journal

_____ , 20 ___

_____
_____
_____
_____

_____ , 20 ___

_____
_____
_____
_____

_____ , 20 ___

_____
_____
_____
_____

Lezione V
I semitoni

5th Lesson
Semitones

Andantino

De - li - ra dub - bio - sa, In -

cɛr - ta va - neg - gia O - gni al - ma che on -

deg - gia Fra i mɔ - ti del _____ cɔr. De -

li - ra dub - bio - sa, In - cɛr - ta va -

Consider replacing the dotted rhythms in this lesson with eighth notes to help
you make sure that you do not insert any pesky H's in your semi-tones.

Legato in Small Intervals

Welcome to Lesson 5 – *I semitoni (Half Steps)*. We can spend a couple chapters here. This is one of the most important lessons and we can use a little time to revisit all our intervals to feel how this lesson informs them. This lesson is a fun exploration of what we started doing all the way back in **Two Notes**. I hope you are still starting every day with your **Daily Exercises**.

The legato semitone is the mother of all legato. Every interval moves through it. *It is the moment when the pitch gives/melts into the new pitch.* It is the moment where you experience the motion of the breath – where you shape the phrase. It is where true drama resides – the pouring forth of the singer's soul. Legato: it is everything.

No use thinking about "where the phrase is going"
if you cannot put together a legato semitone.

As always you can start by singing the lesson on vowels. If you feel your consonant game is on point, go ahead and sing on text immediately. By now the goal is clear, right? De-li-HI-ra dub-bio-HO-sa is not a thing! And do NOT sing straight tone in your desire to sing legato. Keep spinning!

Remember: it is **FREE FLOWING BREATH** that takes you from note to note. Let the pitch follow the breath. Legato is the goal, portamento is what happens when the breath stays in motion (support stays consistent). Support *through* the dotted note into the sixteenth. You are the boss of your dynamics. (Okay, this is weird; I'm saying all the things I imagine I *might* have said if someone was singing! Pick one that might work for you.)

If you want, you can replace the dotted eighth and sixteenth with two eighths to make 100% sure that there is no holding of the breath between the pitches. Remember when we practiced traveling between pitches at different tempos in Lesson 3? Lesson 5 is a good place to continue that practice.

Today we add **Come SWITCH with Me** to our arsenal of exercises to practice laryngeal registration. If you sing **Come YODEL with Me** you are already practicing all the "switch pitches" in both chest and head (falsetto). Now you need to switch on one pitch like advanced singers have already been doing in *Daily Exercises: Laryngeal Registration*. You will soon be a master of this essential skill!

This QR code introduces you to an astonishingly good singer, Rosina Storchio. She was Leoncavallo's first Mimì and Puccini's first Cio-Cio San. Here she is singing *Ah non credea - Ah non giunge* from Bellini's *La sonnambula* in 1911. Listen especially to the easy consistent production of F4 in "light, unpressed chest voice" in the cabaletta.

Switching for treble voices

Switching exercises encourage sopranos and mezzo-sopranos to explore switching between chest and head-dominant production on pitches between C4 and F4. As is often the case in Vaccai (and lots of standard repertoire (for example "Comme autrefois" and the opening of Sophie's "Presentation of the Rose") the first pitch is **anchored in the chest**. There is nothing more satisfying (especially when you are nervous!) than being able to sing these "anchors" confidently in chest without pulling undue attention to it. If Storchio needed that anchor, I think we all do!

Switching for tenors and baritones

These exercises invite the falsetto on E♭4 – G4 to inform your chest-dominant singing to **increase your dynamic range** in the passaggio and simultaneously build a **free and unpressured chest dominant sound**. Repertoire often requires varied dynamics in this range (especially on F4) Examples I can think of include "Il mio tesoro" and "Di provenza". Feel free to experiment with the exercises higher and lower as your easy chest and unreinforced falsetto ranges allow you to do. Only one rule here as everywhere else: Take it one half step at a time! Don't rush the process!

Lesson 5 Grammar

subject
verb
object
adjective
adverb
predicate noun, adv, or adj

prepositional phrase
interjection
conjunction
interrogative pronoun

Delira dubbiosa,
Incerta vaneggia
Ogni alma, che ondeggia
Fra i moti del cor.

Dubbiosa and vaneggia are like 'sollecita' in the first lesson; they are adverbs that look like adjectives

tenors and basses: where in your repertoire might you use more dynamic variation in the passaggio?
treble voices: where might you find "chest anchors" in your repertoire?

_____

_____

_____

_____

_____

_____

Practice Journal

_____ , 20 __

_____

_____

_____

_____

_____

_____

_____ , 20 __

_____

_____

_____

_____

_____

_____ , 20 __

_____

_____

_____

_____

_____

Do NOT push the envelope! Sing only in the range you can achieve ease of production without pushing in either chest or head.

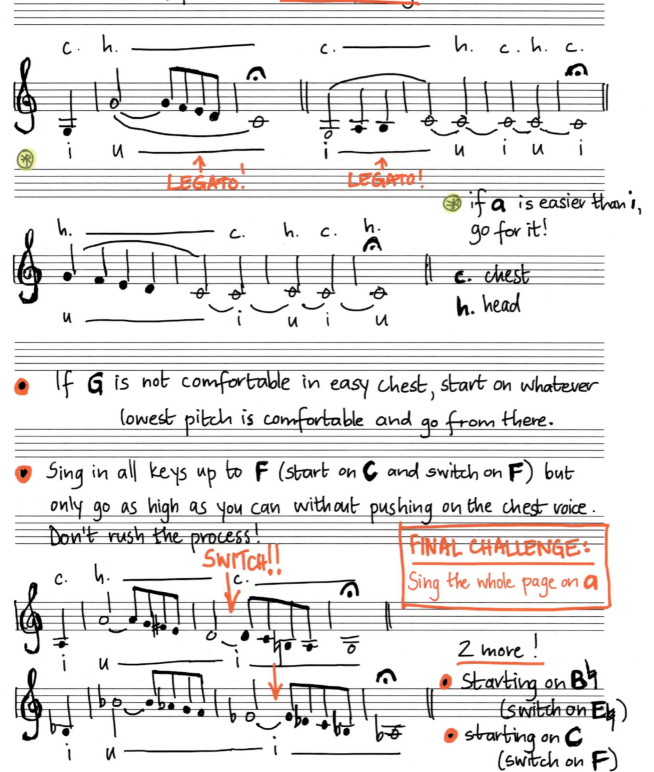

LEGATO! LEGATO!

if **a** is easier than **i**, go for it!

c. chest
h. head

- If **G** is not comfortable in easy chest, start on whatever lowest pitch is comfortable and go from there.

- Sing in all keys up to **F** (start on **C** and switch on **F**) but only go as high as you can without pushing on the chest voice. Don't rush the process!

SWITCH!!

FINAL CHALLENGE:
Sing the whole page on **a**

2 more!
- Starting on B♮ (switch on E♮)
- starting on **C** (switch on **F**)

COME SWITCH WITH ME - TENOR

Do NOT push the envelope! Sing only in the range you can achieve ease of production without pushing in either chest or falsetto.

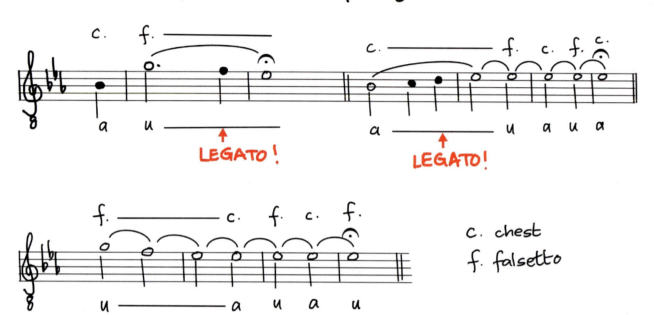

c. chest
f. falsetto

Sing in all keys up to **G** (start on **D** and switch on **G**) but only go as high as you can without reinforcing the falsetto.

DON'T RUSH THE PROCESS! ❤️

one more!
Starting on **D**
(switch on **G**)

Do NOT push the envelope! Sing only in the range you can achieve ease of production without pushing in either chest or falsetto.

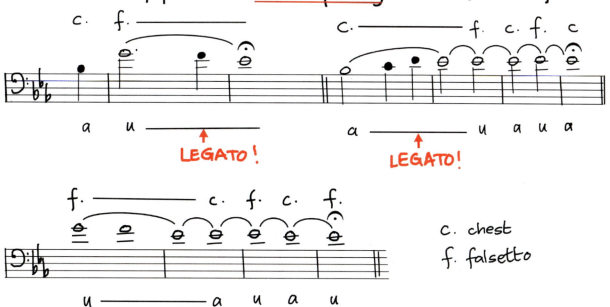

c. chest
f. falsetto

Sing in all keys up to **G** (start on **D** and switch on **G**) but only go as high as you can without reinforcing the falsetto.

DON'T RUSH THE PROCESS!

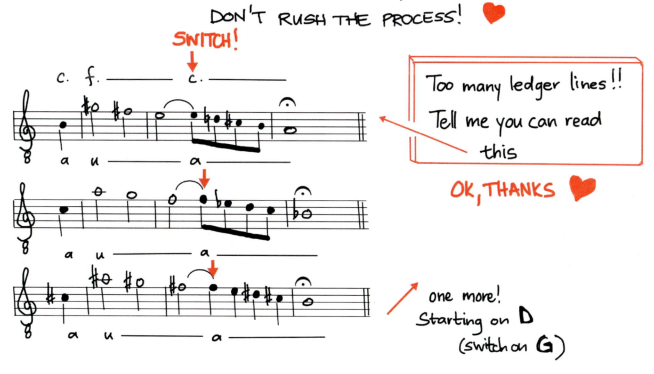

Too many ledger lines!!
Tell me you can read this

OK, THANKS

one more!
Starting on **D**
(switch on **G**)

Dynamics

Let's stick with registration and explore its relationship to dynamics. **Come SOAR and FLOAT with me!** helps you explore registration (dynamics) in and above the passaggio.

Read on if you would like an explanation in words.
Skip to the practice sheet if you prefer!

Note: "Loosey goosey" is my shorthand for
"Don't grip your larynx! Poor thing did nothing to deserve that!"
It does not mean "unstable larynx" of course!

One often hears **sopranos and mezzo-sopranos** comment on how the notes above the upper (secondo) passaggio flourish when the lowest chest tones (G3 to C4) are developed. This is certainly my experience.

> - In chest-dominant production (Mode 1) the vocal folds are short and bulky – they come together like two slabs of meat.
> - In head-dominant production (Mode 2) the vocal folds are stretched and slim – they come together more like two pieces of paper.

How do we find dynamic range above the upper passaggio?

A *floaty top* stays strikingly head-voice dominant with only a *thread of chest* – we stay in that slim, only-paper-touching mode. Try thinking: *Heady with thread of chest.*

To produce a *forte, soaring top* we need to put more of the mass of the vocal folds together. While the vocal folds are stretched, we close them by more engagement of the thyroarytenoids (the "chest voice muscles"). We get more "meaty." Some people like to think: *Add threads of chest.* Others like to think of the thread of chest becoming bulkier. Or you can just think: *Close more.* Or think: *Chest!* even if you are obviously still in head voice. Figure out what works for you.

> We could go further into the precise science, but we can leave it as the fact that chest dominant production has higher closed quotient (percentage of the glottal cycle in which the glottis is closed) – but remember, on A3 this cycle is already happening 220 times per second. You cannot sing with better registration by telling yourself to increase your closed quotient.
>
> **Too. Many. Words. Go play and sing!**

Don't get your mind mired in explanations! You can ignore all of the words and see if the exercise sheet makes enough sense to you on its own. We are looking for the simplest possible way for it to make just enough sense that you get it and can execute. Today's QR code links to **Listen to Dynamics** - be inspired by some fabulous singers exploring all the colors of their voices.

Another plea for non-treble voices to take part in exploring laryngeal registration:

Tenors and baritones/basses need to explore registration if they want an option other than "pedal to the metal" in anything passaggio and above (to be honest, anywhere!) Composers certainly require you to have options. Ignore them at your peril. If by the end of the evening you crash and burn, it is because you ignored dynamics in Act I. Your poor voice is quite literally screaming at you: **ENOUGH ALREADY!** Even though non-treble voice production (these days) is basically chest-dominant, there are no dynamic options without inviting head voice to the party.

Practice Journal

————————— , 20 —

————————— , 20 —

————————— , 20 —

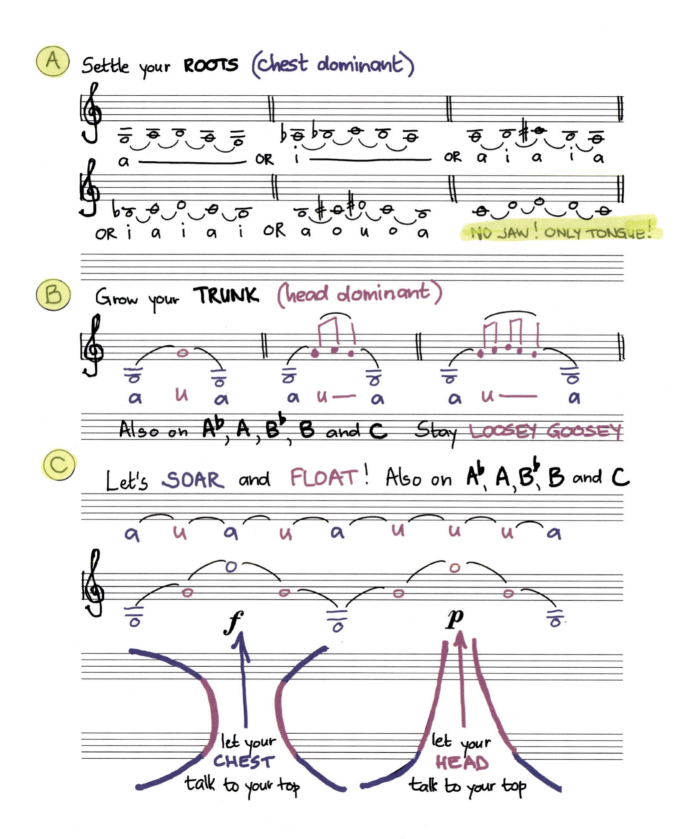

A Settle your **ROOTS** (chest dominant)

- Practice all your vowels and vowel combinations
- Move only what needs to move!

B Grow your **TRUNK** (same dynamic)

Also on **F♯, G, A♭, A** and **B♭**. Stay LOOSEY GOOSEY!

C Let's SOAR and FLOAT! Also on **F♯, G, A♭, A** and **B♭**

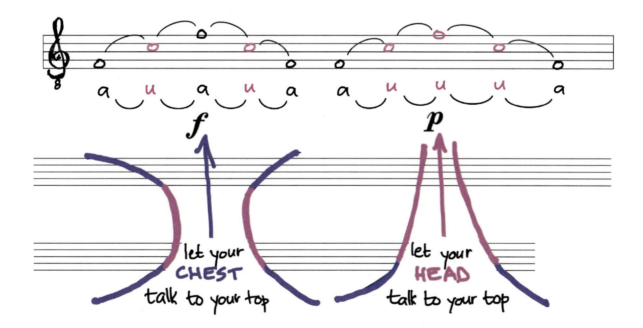

you are not meant to leave chest dominance in this exercise;
rather, find dynamic possibilities within chest dominant sound in the passaggio and above

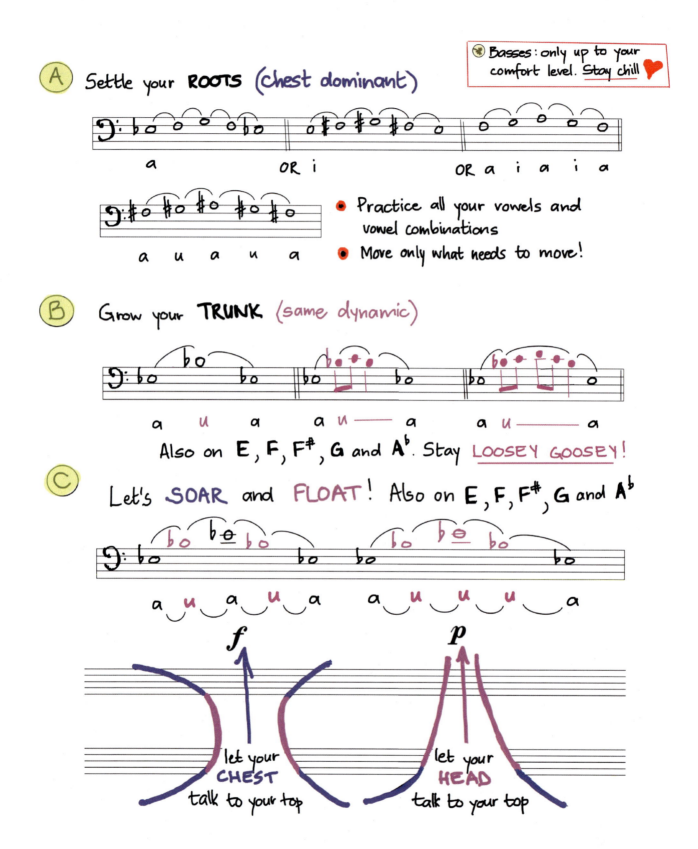

you are not meant to leave chest dominance in this exercise;
rather, find dynamic possibilities within chest dominant sound in the passaggio and above

Guided by Voices Fifty Singers You Should Know 1900–1949

SOPRANO
Frances Alda | Celestina Boninsegna | Kirsten Flagstad | Johanna Gadski | Amelita Galli-Curci | Ria Ginster | Alma Gluck | Lilli Lehmann | Lotte Lehmann

Frida Leider | Claudia Muzio | Antonina Nezhdanova | Rosa Ponselle | Elisabeth Rethberg | Elisabeth Schumann | Bidu Sayão | Rosina Storchio | Ninon Vallin

MEZZO/CONTRALTO
Marian Anderson | Louise Homer | Sigrid Onegin | Ernestine Schumann-Heink | Ebe Stignani | Conchita Supervia | Kerstin Thorborg

TENOR
Jussi Björling | Enrico Caruso | Edmond Clément | André d'Arkor | Beniamino Gigli | Giacomo Lauri-Volpi | Sergei Lemeshev | Giovanni Martinelli | Lauritz Melchior

BARITONE
Aureliano Pertile | Joseph Schmidt | Leonid Sobinov | Pasquale Amato | Mattia Battistini | Giuseppe De Luca | Maurice Renaud | Titta Ruffo | Heinrich Schlusnus | Riccardo Stracciari

BASS
Lawrence Tibbett | Feodor Chaliapin | Alexander Kipnis | Tancredi Pasero | Pol Plançon | Ezio Pinza

Compiled by Steven Tharp

Lezione VI

Modo sincopato

6ᵗʰ Lesson

Syncopation

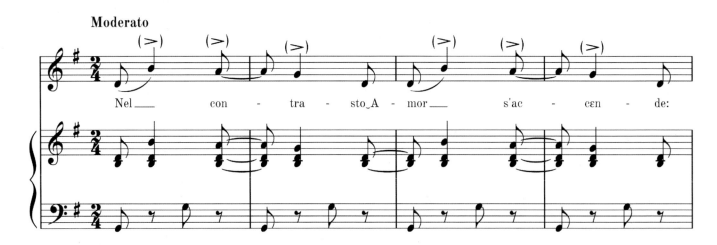

Nel __ con - tra - sto_A - mor __ s'ac - cɛn - de:

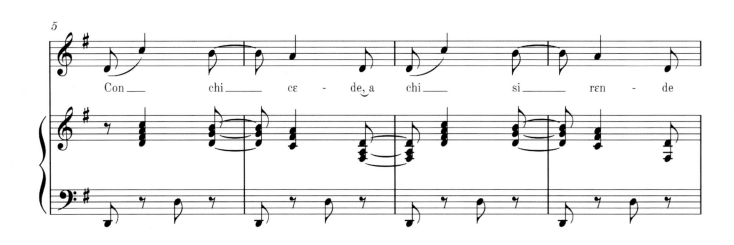

Con __ chi __ cɛ - de, a chi __ si __ rɛn - de

Mai si __ bar - ba - ro non è, mai, __

Review of Studied Skills

One chapter only on Lesson 6, because we want to spend two on Lesson 7: our introduction to singing fast notes! After registration, agility (*moving your voice*), is the most neglected topic these days. My opinion.

At first glance *Nel contrasto Amor s'accende* seems like a silly exercise, right? Syncopation typically shows up a couple of times as a "special effect" in music of this period. Here everything is syncopated - or as we call it in jazz: swinging! Remember that Vaccai set out to train musicianship in addition to building vocal skills. And knowing where the beat is while not singing on it is certainly a useful skill! Can you play the bass line on the beat and sing on the off beat? Get your groove on!

For inspiration here is a QR link to a Harry Connick, Jr. performance teaching his audience about off beats. The audience sadly starts clapping on beats one and three. Harry is not having it and slips in one extra beat to move them to the groovy beats two and four! But we learn more than syncopation here. We review some skills we have worked on:

- After our work on legato semitones this is a good vocalise to extend application of that skill to **intervals of the fifth, sixth, and seventh on one syllable**. Stay smooth in your breath even though the music is syncopated and jaunty. H's are not allowed – not even in syncopation.

- For good measure Vaccai throws in a couple of **semitones** (bars 18 and 27) and **a whole tone** (bar 20) to keep your legato in small intervals on the straight and narrow.

- Our exploration of **registration** continues as well. Sopranos and mezzo-sopranos, see if you can smoothly transition between chest and head. The key of G is a great key to practice this in – it helps you to get C4, D4 and E4 consistently in chest. Pick G♭ or F if you are only comfortable up to E♭4 or D4 in chest. Don't be impatient with yourself. You have plenty of time! Don't push ahead. Go step by step, day by day - or rather half step by half step! Stay process- and not goal-oriented.

I hope you are not getting bored with work on basic skills. When you sing your repertoire, your expressive voice is going to be clearer because of your work here.

I often hear the comment, "A singer must have something to say – he cannot just be technically perfect!" Harrumph! What do they mean by "technically perfect"? I have never heard a beautiful legato-constructed line flow from a singer and thought the singer "had nothing to say".

In my experience, all singers have "something to say" (some more than others, but that is to be expected).

Singers' greatest frustration is inability to sing what they imagine –
being stymied by a technical inefficiency
that distorts delivery of the line they desperately want to bring to life.

Our business is legato and language. We believe improving the singer's confidence in moving freely from note to note, while embracing language as an equal partner, allows the singer to speak (sing) their mind clearly. For us this is "technical perfection" – if such a thing be possible.

Why don't you revisit all the lessons we have done and bring your imagination to life? Read the poem, sing the poem. Just how you imagine it. Let your breath paint each phrase.

THE NOTATION IS NOT THE MUSIC

Does your poetry study and understanding of legato allow you to see the things that cannot be notated? Are you using all the colors you discover in your daily *messa di voce* exercises? As you expand your skills, remember to check in with your imagination.

PAINT WITH ALL YOUR COLORS
SING EXACTLY WHAT YOU IMAGINE

Lesson 6 Grammar

| subject |
| verb |
| object |
| adjective |
| adverb |
| predicate noun, adv, or adj |

| prepositional phrase |
| interjection |
| conjunction |
| interrogative pronoun |

Nel contrasto Amor s' accende ;
Con chi cede , a chi s' arrende
Mai si barbaro non è.

Which cantabile arias and songs are benefitting from my daily exercises?

_____

_____

_____

_____

_____

Practice Journal

——————— , 20 ——

_____

_____

_____

_____

_____

_____

——————— , 20 ——

_____

_____

_____

_____

_____

_____

——————— , 20 ——

_____

_____

_____

_____

_____

_____

Lezione VII

Introduzione alle volate

Questa lezione si comincerà col prendere il tempo Adagio poi si affretterà fine all'Allegro secondo l'abilità dell'allievo.

7th Lesson

Introduction to Coloratura

Start this lesson Adagio and increase the tempo until you get to Allegro according to your ability.

Co - me il can - do - re D'in - tat - ta ne - ve è d'un bel co - re La fe - del - tà: Un' or - ma so - la. Che in sé ri - ce - ve. Tut - ta le in - vo - la La sua bel - tà. Tut - ta le in - vo - la La sua bel - tà.

Singing Fast Starts with Singing Slowly

Welcome to *Introduzione alle volate* – preparation for singing fast notes. We will spend a while here. It is worth exploring in detail how singing slow legato intervals translates to singing coloratura. When someone asks me about singing with a metronome, I recoil in horror! Now, I know that many people disagree with me, but I am here to tell you that I have never seen a singer truly get better at singing fast notes by whipping his voice with an unrelenting, annoying beat.

We are often asked, "How do I get my voice to move better and faster?" and the first part of the answer is always, **"By moving it slowly and smoothly."** We are not the first one to offer this advice. Read what Vaccai says at the top of the page: "Start this lesson Adagio and increase the tempo until you get to Allegro according to your ability." And he does not mean "according to the your ability to press ▲ on your metronome!"

A five note diatonic scale is simply a construction of our old friends, the tone and the semitone – or if you haven't figured out already, whole steps and half steps by another name. We have practiced the building blocks of good scale singing already.

Resist the urge to sing this exercise fast today. I know you don't WANT to resist this urge. Please DO resist it if you need or want to improve your coloratura ability. Let's practice concentrating on having all the intervals smoothly connected on the breath attaining all our goals we have solidified by now.

- Sing legato between the sixteenth notes – there is not one single H in the whole poem. Nor does H make a sound in Italian.
- Keep the vowel pure with an easy, "soft" tongue - tongue tension will kill your coloratura.
- Monitor your jaw movement to make sure it is not articulating for you.
- Check in with your whole body – right arm, left big toe – your brain, breath, and your vocal folds are at work. Don't attempt to change pitch by lifting your shoulders!

DO hear the pitches BEFORE you sing.

If you are not going to "articulate" the pitches with aspiration, your tongue or your jaw, where does the clarity come from? THE EAR. We are not talking about "listening to yourself" like an audience member. We are talking about **audiating pitches** before you sing them.

If you can HEAR FAST, you can SING FAST.

Singers are often told, "Don't listen to yourself." The sad byproduct of this is putting their audiating ear under lock and key as well. This "inner ear" is essential to singing coloratura. By the way, it is also essential in clean onset and "picking a color." You should not sing without imagination — we talked about that in the previous chapter as well.

For the singer the most important part of imagination is hearing the pitch before singing it. And hearing it precisely.

Another way of explaining this: you cannot expect your body to achieve a goal if you do not set a specific one. DO imagine perfection, and then DO NOT despair if you do not achieve it all the time. Bob Rotella taught me how to help a singer marry these two concepts in his book *Golf Is Not a Game of Perfect*. I have learned so much from him! He is a genius and you should definitely read this gem. You can listen to some conversations we've had about Rotella in **Singer's Mindset** on **The Gym Floor**.

Sing the lesson slowly, hearing the pitches before you sing them.

If you want to explore getting a little faster without giving up on the legato, go for it! But know that we are going to explore legato coloratura in the old Italian way. Unfortunately, many people who are famous for singing coloratura repertoire today do not sing legato coloratura — part of the long story that reduces to: bel canto and baroque operas disappear from the repertory, generations of singers learn to sing in a verismo style, and then suddenly have to "keep up" with the precision expected in bel canto without ever having studied the skills. We're here to learn those once-abandoned skills. In the next chapter I will share some tips on increasing velocity without that darn metronome. **For now, step one of singing fast is singing slowly.**

Today we listen to another *Guided by Voices* video produced by Steven Tharp. The video is designed to help opera lovers fall in love just by listening. In a world where increasing emphasis is put on the visual, it is easy for opera's newcomers to lose their ears in the razzle-dazzle of modern opera productions.

Of course Muzio is not perfect – none of us are or ever will be! I wish her sixteenth note groups were more languid and less marcato, but still she brings a tear to my eye. I would like to think that she would have enjoyed being part of our community. I can almost see her post in a BCBC Facebook practice group:

"Ugh, I wish I expressed as much freedom in the shorter notes as I do in the longer ones – I'll play with that idea tomorrow.
Thank you, fellow Boot Campers, for your support and encouragement."

Lesson 7 Grammar

Come il candore
D' intatta neve
È d' un bel core
La fedeltà.

notice how the **subject** doesn't come until the end of the poem

what fast Repertoire do you commit to practicing slowly?

_____

_____

_____

Practice Journal

—————————— , 20 —

_____

_____

_____

—————————— , 20 —

_____

_____

_____

—————————— , 20 —

_____

_____

_____

Here we go! *"How do I get my voice to move?"* This chapter is also for those of you who might be singing non-legato coloratura (aspirated or muscularly manipulated in some way) and are interested in exploring the old ways with us. In the previous chapter we explored the most important lesson of all in singing fast:

SINGING FAST STARTS WITH SINGING SLOWLY

And then you sing faster *without changing how you sing*. Yes, there are many modern singers who seem to think something changes when the notes have more flags – they contort their faces and jaws, move their heads, "lighten up" on their support, put an accent on every beat. Okay, some do these things when singing slowly as well. What a world! But if your voice is properly trained and your musicianship skills are up to snuff

YOU DO NOT NEED TO GAIN A SECOND TECHNIQUE
(AND ABANDON THE ONE YOU ALREADY HAVE) TO SING COLORATURA

We are now entering the part of Vaccai that deals with ornaments, and all coloratura passages are by definition ornamental: ornamental in the sense that they are constructed of

PATTERNS EXPLORING A SKELETON

- The singer uses these patterns to **ornament** the often bare-bone *melodic skeleton* of slow melodies in the early Italian style – think *Ombra mai fu*. Later in the course we will look at how Mozart's *Ach, ich fühl's* would look like if we deconstruct the ornaments he wrote for his Pamina.

- In fast Baroque arias and the bel canto *cabaletta*, composers use these very same patterns to create coloratura passages; singers are called upon to **vary** the patterns in the repeat of the *cabaletta* by filling out the *harmonic skeleton* in their own way.

We ORNAMENT slow, melodic music – decorating an existing melody
We VARY coloratura passages – substituting patterns to fit the harmony

In upcoming chapters we will explore all these building blocks of ornamentation and coloratura by exploring in isolation all the riffs your voice can do:

- scales ("trains of passing tones")
- appoggiaturas
- acciaccaturas
- mordents
- turns
- trills
- flips (*our shorthand for coloratura patterns jumping to other chord tones, usually intervals of the third or the fourth*)

Anna Maria Pellegrini Celoni (1780-1835)
Grammatica (1810)

Variations ↑

Skeleton

Figured Bass

Celoni's "Grammatica" is a concise treatise filled with
fantastically useful exercises. Chronologically she fits
between the oft-quoted Corri and García and thus
provides invaluable information about the continuum
of the Italian style.

○ appoggiatura/acciaccatura

ᴍ mordent

→ scale (passing tones)

∿ turns

∨ flips

flips created by
rearranged pitches
of the turn

Here is the master Celoni at work showing us how to flesh out a skeleton and practice singing coloratura all at the same time. Exciting, right?! Think about the coloratura passages in your arias simply as combinations of these patterns, learn to execute them smoothly, and then voilà! You can sing fast! We refer to these patterns as

UNITS OF PITCHES

So now that I have you excited, we return to Lesson 7 and the five-note scale. First things first! Here are some ways you can improve your ability to sing this lesson (or any coloratura passage) faster without committing the sins discussed in the previous chapter:

- You already know number one. **Sing it** *adagio* **and with smooth legato. Always come back to number one.** This is where you check in to make sure every pitch is secure both in your ear and in your voice. Nothing will derail your coloratura singing more than an iffy pitch somewhere. It is amazing how many people skip returning to this step after they "learned the notes."

- While singing slowly, **think about WHAT you are singing**. "Come il candore" exercises the most often used pattern in coloratura: a scale (or part of a scale) which is formed by **filling in the spaces between chord tones with passing tones**. In this vocalise, the first and third note of each group are chord tones and the second and fourth are passing tones. While it is simple in this lesson, this concept is important for the audiating ear.

- We are going to ask our ear to start hearing multiple pitches *at the same time – in groups* in order to allow our voices to move more quickly. It is essential to know where the consonant and dissonant tones occur – especially when our UNITS OF PITCHES become more complicated. Welcome to **Harmony for Singers!**

Another way to think about this is that you don't have time to construct the line interval by interval like when you sing slow music:

We will have to learn to hear groups of pitches
and train our voices to execute these groups in one flowing motion.

Note: If you are tired today,
close the book and come back tomorrow.
The following information is essential –
make sure you give yourself time
to grasp the chapter fully.

If you're up for it, turn the page!

FIND THE SKELETON

1. Make an exercise for your coloratura passage by singing only the chord tones (the skeleton). Make sure that they stay smoothly connected on the breath. Consider returning to Lesson 1 and sing the Lesson on Thirds on one vowel. This skeleton is in pink on the practice sheet. Do it all through the lesson, discovering the skeleton for yourself once it is not written.

2. Even though this lesson is easy to sing, this is a good place to learn how to practice in rhythm without abandoning our mantra: **ONE BREATH IMPULSE PER PHRASE.** Many people use rhythms but jerk their breath around and put random accents. How can singing on and off the breath be a good exercise?! Stop it! Try to sing a dotted rhythm (long/short→ long/short→long) on each of the coloratura figures while keeping your breath smoothly engaged, thus singing with continuous dynamic and vibrato. This is the **red rhythm** on the practice sheet. Do it all through the lesson.

Note: It is essential that you feel that what happens after a beat belongs to the next beat. Including across a bar line! One of the great sadnesses of music making: lingering across a bar line. If I ever teach kids, I will cut up two apples when I teach them notation of rhythm: the second half of Apple A belongs with Apple B! The AND part of one-AND-two belongs with two, not one! One...and→two. Ok, the thought of my teaching kids is frightening, I know! The rules of rhythmic notation bind everything in one beat together neatly. While it is effective in a rudimentary way, it leads us visually to think IN beats instead of BETWEEN beats.

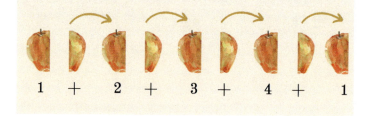

3. Next we do the blue rhythm on the practice sheet all through the lesson: expanding the unit of pitches we hear before releasing our bodies to execute it. I don't care if you have to stay on the long note for 5 seconds (or longer!). The important thing is that you are able to hear **the unit of three fast notes and their arrival on the next beat** before you sing them ("release your body to sing them"). Remember: ain't no metronome whipping you here! You are singing "according to your ability" as Vaccai puts it. I'm adding, "according to your ability to audiate."

In this moment you want to start experiencing with what I call **marcato with the ear, legato with the breath.** You must hear the pitches CLEARLY with the ear and then allow the breath to connect them SMOOTHLY. **Articulation of the pitches originates in the ear.** It is of the utmost importance that in the absence of the dreaded H's or tongue or jaw motion, the ear articulates effectively.

4. Last step is to explore at what tempos you can sing Lesson 7 while always keeping your audiating ear just a step ahead. Don't expect your body to sing something your mind has not imagined yet.

Enjoy some first rate old-style coloratura by scanning today's QR code!

Think TA-KA-TA-KA-TA or DU-BI-DU-BI-DU but sing AAAAAAA!

Sometimes it can be fun actually singing these syllables in Step 4! There is a good reason jazz singers scat on versions of du-bi-du-bi-du: separating the pitches with voiced plosives and alternating vowels allows their audience to hear the pitches they are imagining very clearly. Simultaneously it allows them to keep their breath moving freely because you cannot scat if you interrupt your breath. It would interrupt the flow of the imagination (audiating ear). Good coloratura is just like that.

Note: if the coloratura starts on the 2nd sixteenth after a tied (long) note as it often does, start with BI: DUUUUU (long note)-BI-DU-BI-DU-BI, etc.

I don't believe in muscle memory. You are not going to sing spectacular coloratura because it will "become a habit." If excellence could be achieved by mindlessly repeating a habit, more people would be excellent. Singing hard coloratura is nothing like brushing your teeth.

I believe in muscles trained to execute what the brain tells them to do.

THE BRAIN STAYS ENGAGED AND THE MASTER OF THE BODY

I have spent most of my adult life dealing with the singer's brain. You cannot leave that thing to think whatever it wants! And you cannot get it to stop thinking either! Nor should you! Stop telling yourself that thinking is bad. **Thinking unhelpful thoughts is bad.** Googling around your brain is bad even if the thousand things in there are all good. Judging yourself is bad. Using your brain to set a clear, simple goal for your body and being able to execute it is **technique** and

TECHNIQUE IS THE VEHICLE OF EXPRESSION

KEYBOARD HARMONY FOR SINGERS

Come PIANO with Me inspires you to see harmony first. Do you know what the chords are? Play them in their simplest form (the black block chords in the practice sheet). If you want to get fancy, you can practice all the oom-pah versions of bel canto accompaniments. It is fun to be able to accompany yourself! Yes, you can sit and sing. You know some director is going to make you do it soon...

COLORATURA PRACTICE RHYTHMS

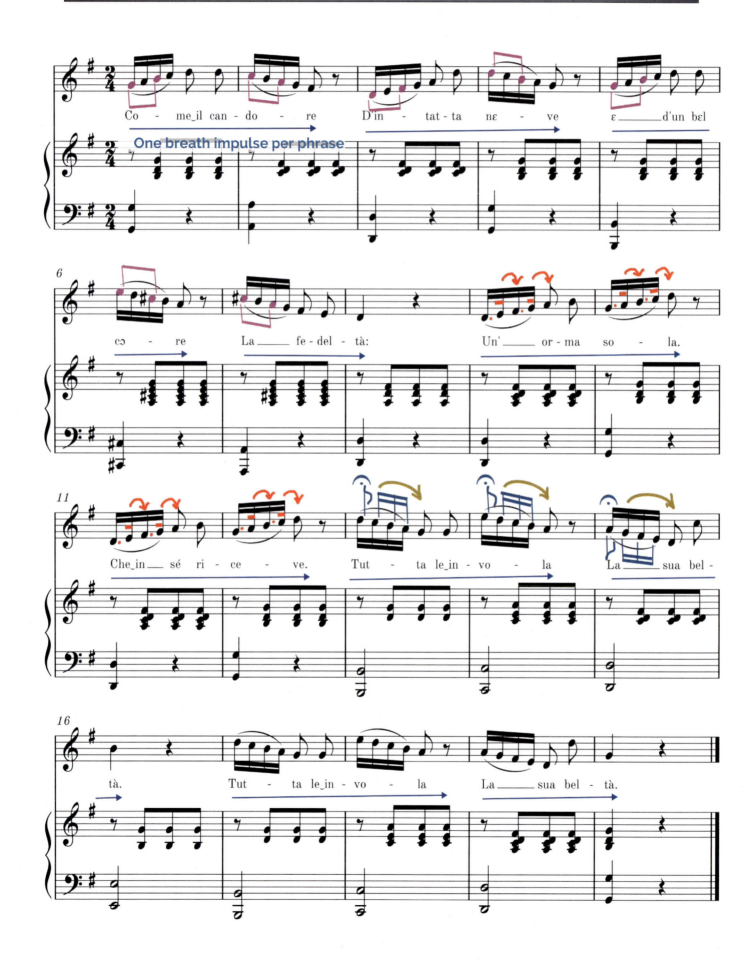

COME PIANO WITH ME

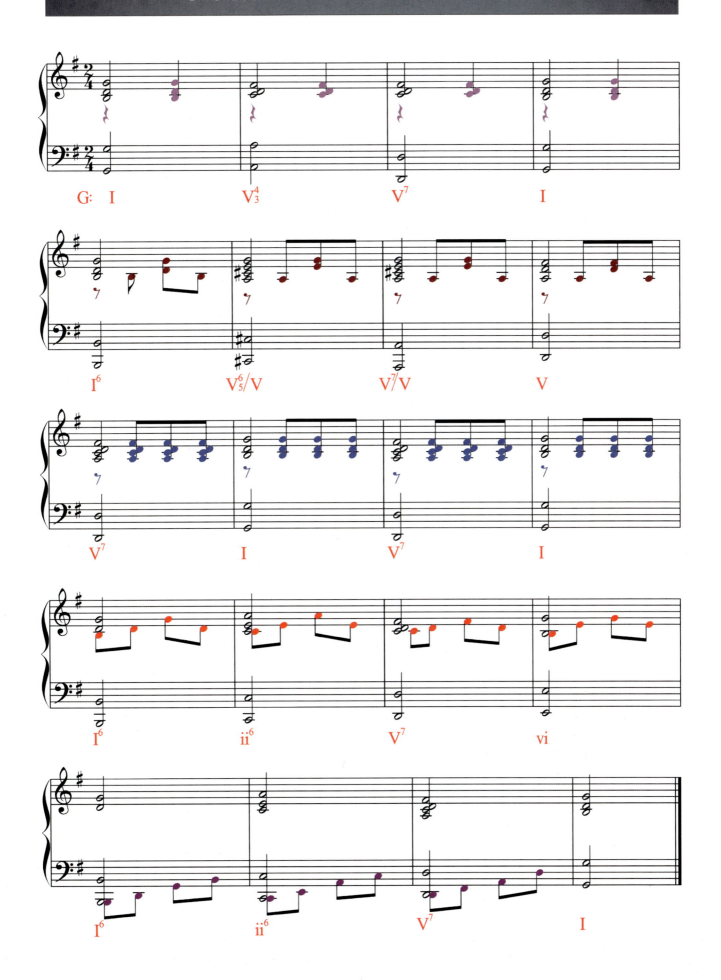

Practice Journal

————————— , 20 —

_____

_____

_____

_____

_____

————————— , 20 —

_____

_____

_____

_____

_____

————————— , 20 —

_____

_____

_____

_____

_____

_____

What fast repertoire have you avoided in the past that you might consider tackling now?

_____

_____

_____

_____

_____

We have seen before how Latin's morphing into Italian resulted in the Italian phenomenon of phrasal doubling. Let us examine the complication of syntax or word order in poetic Italian as another "receipt" or after-effect of the Latin > Italian story.

Latin is a synthetic and inflectional language: synthetic because each individual word can transform to convey the role it plays in the sentence, and **inflectional** because the word stems change or acquire endings to indicate gender, number, and case (whether it is a subject, direct/indirect object, indicator of possession, etc). Word order in Latin is not important, because each individual word contains all the information about what role it plays in the sentence.

A common illustration involves Marius and Claudius. When we want to say that **Marius** saw Claud**ius** in Latin, we have to say that **Marius** vidit Claud**ium**– why did this change? Claudius is the recipient of the action (Marius's seeing him); in other words, Claudius is the 'direct object.' Therefore Claudius must be declined into the accusative case by changing *-us* to *-um*. in Latin we can say:

MARI**US**	VIDIT	CLAUD**IUM**	Subject-Verb- Object
CLAUD**IUM**	VIDIT	MARI**US**	O-V-S
CLAUD**IUM**	MARI**US**	VIDIT	O-S-V
VIDIT	CLAUD**IUM**	MARI**US**	V-O-S
VIDIT	MARI**US**	CLAUD**IUM**	V-S-O
MARI**US**	CLAUD**IUM**	VIDIT	S-O-V

All six of which are rendered in Italian as **Mario vide Claudio**.

Dramatic poetry in the period we are studying required librettists and poets to change word order in Italian to protect the poetic form and rhyme scheme. This results in confusing constructions to the modern eye and ear. For English speakers who have studied Shakespeare, think back to sentences like, "And in such eyes as ours appear not faults" which might more clearly be rendered "Faults do not appear in such eyes as ours." The task of the librettist is to craft dramatic poetry that conveys action without seeming colloquial – variation in syntax offers the librettist both more opportunity to refine the individual character's voice and to craft more memorable poetry since the text does not resemble normal speech.

The next page contains some of the confusing lessons from Vaccai put into what, for English speakers, looks more like "normal word order."

Manca sollecita
dies   quickly

Più dell' usato,
more. than. usual

Ancor che s' agiti
even though   it be stirred

Con lieve fiato,
by delicate breeze/breath

Face che palpita
flame   that   flickers

Presso al morir.
close   to dying/death.

(Una) face che palpita presso al morir
A flame that flickers close to death

manca più sollecita(mente) dell'usato,
dies   more   quickly   than usual

ancor che (ancorché) s'agiti con lieve fiato.
even if   it be stirred with gentle breath.

Come il candore
like   the purity

D' intatta neve
of untouched   snow

È d' un bel core
is of   a good/virtuous heart

La fedeltà.
the loyalty/fidelity.

La fedeltà d'un bel c(u)ore
The loyalty of a virtuous heart

è come il candore d'intatta neve.
is like   the purity of untouched snow.

---

try this exercise on a poem from your repertoire

_____   _____

_____   _____

_____   _____

_____   _____

_____   _____

_____   _____

_____   _____

_____   _____

Practice Journal

——————— , 20 ——

_____

_____

_____

_____

_____

——————— , 20 ——

_____

_____

_____

_____

_____

——————— , 20 ——

_____

_____

_____

_____

_____

Lezione VIII

Le appoggiature sopra e sotto

L'Appoggiatura è il miglior ornamento del Canto, il di cui effetto dipende dal darle il suo giusto valore. Non sarà però difetto l'accrescerlo, quanto lo sarebbe il diminuirlo.

8th Lesson

The Appoggiatura Above and Below

The appoggiatura is the best ornament in song, whose effect depends on giving it its correct value. It would never, however, be wrong to lengthen its value, as it would be to shorten it.

Sεn - za l'a - ma - bi - le Dio di Ci - tε - ra I ___ dì non tor - na - no Di ___ pri - ma - vε - ra. Non spi - ra un zε - fi - ro, Non spun - ta un fior. L'εr - be sul mar - gi - ne Del fon - te_a - mi - co,

* Refer to the NOTE at the end of the next chapter for an explanation of our rhythmic notation here.

The Appoggiatura

Time to delve into the history of the appoggiatura. Welcome to *Senza l'amabile Dio di Citera*. Three chapters on just the appoggiatura because we have lots of facts to cover. Acciaccaturas will have to wait a while. For today we are going to keep it very simple and explain the *why* of the appoggiatura in one sentence:

The dissonance of the appoggiatura and its resolution support the stressed and unstressed syllables of the poem.

This is why it is sometimes referred to as the **prosodic appoggiatura**; prosody is the rhythm, stress, and intonation of words as they are strung together. One more reason why it is important to be on top of your poetry game!

Let's look at the poem of Lesson 8:

Senza l'amabile
Dio di Citera
I di non tornano
Di primavera.
Non spira un zefiro,
Non spunta un fior.

L'erbe sul margine
Del fonte amico,
Le piante vedove
Sul colle aprico
Per lui rivestono
L'antico onor.

Note: The appoggiatura does double duty: it does occur as a melodic ornament, but here we concentrate on **the prosodic appoggiatura**, which results from poetic stress. This is a useful distinction to make when dealing with people saying they "don't like" a specific appoggiatura. If the appoggiatura is prosodic, likes and dislikes are not on the table. The appoggiatura must happen – research into historically informed performance practice tells us.

If you want to be HIPP you must sing your prosodic appoggiaturas - all of them!

Can you see where the **poetic accent** in each *quinario* falls? Can you see that those accents correspond to **strong beats** in the music? Can you see how the inherent rhythm of the *piano* and *sdrucciolo* endings of the poetic lines leave the composer with **multiple syllables on the same pitch**?

This is an inherent "problem" of any language that scans like this: the new harmony has arrived on the stressed syllable, but, oops! there is another unstressed syllable (or two) to sing! The Italians solved this problem with the appoggiatura, and as you will see in our quote compilation on page 122, the Germans and French followed suit.

If you look at the one sentence explanation above, can you see how the dissonance of the appoggiaturas on the stressed syllables of the *piano* and *sdrucciolo* endings support the lingual rhythm and poetic meter? In the absence of these dissonances those syllables would all seem similarly stressed unless of course you decided to sing the unstressed syllables softer or, God forbid, off the voice.

Raise your hand if you have been told "not to sit on the last syllable"?

The problem lies not with the "last syllable" but with what comes before it. The Italians ask you to sit (lean/appoggiare) on the stressed syllable – on the penultimate syllable in the case of a piano word, or antepenultimate in the case of a sdrucciolo word. If you "sit" on this syllable, and if you "sit" on an appoggiatura you won't be prone to sitting on the last syllable!

"Stressed and "unstressed" syllables

These are common terms used to describe the syllables in poetic feet. From a singer perspective it is better to execute **"long" and "short"** since it is clearly not a good idea to sing every second syllable softer and end each phrase with a diminuendo! Your prosody comes from the inflection of the language. The inflection is supported by the dissonance of the appoggiatura. It is essentially Italian to support your voice through long and short syllables alike. Italians can even say final syllables louder than the preceding syllable, but NEVER longer. **Avoid the note "Your recitative is too sung" by singing it more!** Support all of it consistently and you want sound sing-songy!

Can you see how it makes sense that the strophes end in *tronco*? How satisfying it is to arrive at **fior** and on**or** and NOT have to put appoggiaturas? It really feels that you arrived! How amazing that the arrival back to the tonic chord (or new tonic if you modulated) inspired poets to apocopate the final word of the strophe if it was not tronco to begin with. Does this makes sense? If the strophes ended with the piano words "fiore" and "onore" we would have had to place yet more appoggiaturas. If you look back at Lesson 7 Metastasio avoided apocopation by ending strophes with words that are already tronco: fedel**tà** and bel**tà**.

Why did they not just write it?!

The convention of **not** notating the appoggiatura has its roots in the conventions of writing for the continuo group (low strings and harpsichord or fortepiano). In addition to the convention of notating recitative in $\frac{4}{4}$ time, it was customary in recitative to

- place the stressed syllables of the poem on beats one and three,
- arrive at new harmonies on those same beats if a new harmony was required, and
- write only consonant pitches on those beats in order to clarify the implied harmony for the continuo group.

Remember that those players only had the bass line and the vocal line, and notation of the dissonant appoggiatura would **confuse the eye as to what harmony to provide**. Cool, right?

Recognizing where to place the appoggiatura was considered part of basic instruction. Don't believe me? You can get it straight from the horses' mouths in **Appoggiaturas through the Ages**, my collection of quotes from the baroque to the bel canto eras at the end of this chapter.

The convention of the prosodic appoggiatura applies to all of Handel, Mozart, Rossini, Donizetti (who notates them inconsistently), Bellini (who notates them always), and Verdi (who is the first one to actively step away from this tradition as his genius leads him down ever more modern paths of melody and harmony). Our quotes provide examples only for the German and French repertoire since we will spend much time discussing Italian examples for the rest of the course.

Often quoted as proof of the prevalence of the prosodic appoggiatura is a recitative between Rigoletto and Sparafucile. Verdi creates a thoroughly modern and stark effect by asking the singer NOT to sing the customary appoggiaturas. He goes further yet and eliminates the

"This recitative to be sung without the customary appoggiaturas"

third from the chord in the orchestra leaving it up to the voice to define the harmony. An eerie, other-worldly sound is created. Verdi is busy doing something new. This has nothing to do with tradition.

Note: Even though by the time of *Rigoletto* the notated appoggiatura was becoming the norm, Verdi still realized that the singer might add the non-notated appoggiatura unless specifically requested to refrain from doing so.

As Corri teaches us (see quote sheet), the convention applies not only to recitative, but to musical numbers alike. The continuo group was hard at work in those as well. Composers started to notate the appoggiatura when the continuo group fell out of fashion and everything including recitatives was accompanied by the orchestra (often just the string section). As soon as nobody would have been confused by notated dissonance, composers went ahead and started writing the dissonant note. How ironic that the notation intended to clarify the harmony for the keyboardist is the very thing that confuses the modern singer's eyes. More in the next chapter when we look at Corri in a little more detail.

For now, speak the poem, sing the lesson and feel how satisfying it is to *lean into the dissonance on the prosodic accent.* Achieve this by lengthening the dissonant pitch (and stressed syllable).

**To be clear: the notated appoggiatura (the "small" note)
replaces the notated consonant (the "big" note) completely.**

There are ways to vary the appoggiatura and we will get to them with the help of García in due course. For now just practice the regular old appoggiatura! Vaccai has shown you where.

Note: Please sing "**spi**ra", "**zef**firo", "**spun**ta", "**lu**i" and "ri**ves**tono" with the correct prosodic accent. The written rhythms of the final piano and sdrucciolo words of the phrase (long note on an unstressed syllable) are a notational convention. Sing the stressed syllables long and with appoggiaturas, regardless of the rhythmic notation. The long syllables of "Non **spi**ra ... un **zef**firo ... Non **spun**ta ... un **fior**" should all feel and sound the same. Review poetry posts if you are not yet clear on the fact that piano, sdrucciolo and tronco words occupy similar rhythmic space.

Practice Journal _____ , 20 __

_____

_____

_____

_____

_____ , 20 __

_____

_____

_____

_____

_____ , 20 __

_____

_____

_____

_____

If the scholar be well instructed in this, the appoggiaturas will become so familiar to him by continual practice, that by the time he is come out of his first lessons, he will laugh at those composers that mark them, with a design either to be thought "modern" or to shew that they understand the art of singing better than the singers. Poor Italy: pray tell me; do not the singers now-a-days know where the appoggiaturas are to be made, unless they are pointed at with a finger? In my time their own knowledge shewed it them.

Tosi: *Observations on the Florid Song*, 1743

In Recitative it is to be remembered that it should not follow an equal beat, but rather to be sung following the content of the Poetry, sometimes slower or faster. On top of that, singers must take into account that they must not always sing the notes as they are notated, rather, every now and again should use what are known as Accents.

Telemann: *Harmonischer Gottesdienst*, 1725/6

Indeed, either an air, or recitative, sung exactly as it is commonly noted, would be a very inexpressive, nay, a very uncouth performance; for not only the respective duration of the notes is scarcely even hinted at, but one note is frequently marked instead of another, as is the case where a note is repeated, instead of that note with its proper appoggiatura or grace... in consequence of which, the singer is misled, by being made to sing a wrong note.

Corri: A *Select Collection of Songs and Duetts from Operas in the Highest Esteem*, 1780

The Italians, in their method of singing Recitative, have as a principle to change certain notes, for the purpose of giving more elegance and taste to its simple and uniform melody. We believe that one ought to adopt this method everywhere, with certain restrictions. Here are various examples of passages in which the Italians practice this changing of notes. In examining attentively these same examples, one will see that these changes are not made except on a note that is repeated, and that one consistently changes these notes only on the strong beats and never on the weak beats of the musical phrase.

Mengozzi: *Méthode de chant*, 1804

Mengozzi marked the appoggiaturas **after** the note which they replace, unlike most composers

It is customary in recitative to use a small note or appoggiatura placed above and in place of the first (note) on the strong beat of the measure. This appoggiatura, of which the following examples will illustrate the usage, gives the grace and melody of the recitative.

Garaudé: *Méthode complète de chant*, 1825

When the first two notes of a bar terminate a member of a phrase the first always bears the prosodic accent and for that reason it is necessary to convert it into an appoggiatura... the effect of the two equal notes would not be tolerable.

García: *A Complete Treatise on the Art of Singing* Part II, 1847

How do we know what we know ?

I am often asked, "Well, how can you be so sure how singers sang in Mozart's time?! There were no recordings!" Recordings are only one way we gather information about the past. While recorded sound is an incredibly useful tool, it only reaches back so far into history.

How can we look further back yet?

Beyond recordings there are two other main ways we "know what we know." Today, we will consider one of them in a little more detail: **historical treatises**. We quoted quite a few of them in **Appoggiaturas through the Ages** already and have been referring to them on topics other than the appoggiatura consistently.

To understand why the Italians (and others) started to write about the conventions of Italian style, we have to understand just how powerful the Italians were. **Italian opera was the name of the game.** It was immensely popular, and very early on, the Italian tradition became an international one. Some of the leading composers of the Italian tradition were not born in Italy. To think that Handel, Glück, and Mozart were writing in something different than the "Italian style," would be, to say the least, a misconception.

Beyond composers' embracing of the style, we see the establishment of Italian opera houses around the world – London, Paris, New York, to name some big ones. As the Italian operatic tradition spread, Italians moved all over the world both as singers and instructors. London, especially, had a tremendous influx of Italian maestri. It was in fashion to have young ladies taught "the Italian style of singing" by an Italian. A lot of what we know comes from Italian manuals on singing for foreigners. Corri is one of them.

Domenico Corri moved to Scotland around 1781 and to London around 1790 where he died in 1825. He was a pupil of Porpora who in turn was a student of Scarlatti. Porpora had some other famous students including the superstar castrato Farinelli. Reading Corri puts us in touch with quite a bit of history – the sound of which could not yet be recorded, but nevertheless about which much was written. Corri is best known for writing the **The Singer's Preceptor** or Treatise on Vocal Music, but the quote on Appoggiaturas through the Ages is from the preface to his first volume of **A Select Collection of Songs and Duetts from Operas in the Highest Esteem.**

Example II from Corri's Introduction to his *Collection* is often reproduced to illustrate how singers were to "interpret" the written notes. Music notation was (and still is) ever evolving, adhering to different conventions in different eras. There is no virtue in believing that the score is sacred if you don't commit to the study of the true meaning of the symbols according to the period in which they were written.

We have already discussed in detail how rhythmic notation displays but one level of rhythm, expecting the sophisticated singer to infuse it with additional information gleaned from poetic meter. We continue to discover how the pitch notation similarly provides a blueprint to be explored and ornamented (or varied) by the performer. We become true collaborators with the composer.

It is important that we introduce you to the sources, both so that you know we remain fact-based, and so that you can delve further into them if you wish.

You will hear many opinions in your singing career; challenging a fact with an opinion is like bringing a knife to a gunfight. Read Corri, and be suitably prepared.

We study Corri's artifact of how *Che farò senza Euridice* should (or could) go. The "could" part refers to you using these ornaments to inspire your own. Really, we already have *Regnava nel silenzio* with only one set of variations. The world does not need to be subjected to another "I have ornaments but they are the same as everybody else's, because we all bought the same book" experience. Don't worry! We'll have you on your way to writing your own ornaments from your own imagination for your own voice in no time.

I have been responsible for disagreements in many a voice studio when saying "If you sing the notes (and, God help us, the rhythms!) exactly as you see them in the Schirmer anthology, you are singing something, but not an aria by Glück!" We find Corri's helpful guide to this aria in the same volume quoted above. Guadagni (the famous castrato who originated the role of Orfeo) sang excerpts from the opera in London in the 1770/1 season. Corri's book was published in 1779/1780.

For now, just concentrate on the appoggiaturas. I clarify which are not obligatory on the score and will discuss this in more detail in the next chapter. You will also see some appoggiatura variations and additional ornamental ideas which we will discuss in later chapters. Don't turn ahead!

How amazing it would be if we could free this aria from the confines of consonance, strict $\frac{4}{4}$ time and accompanying chords being played in the wrong place. More about this as well as time progresses – for now, just believe me and Corri that convention was to separate orchestra from voice in accompagnatos as much as possible.

In the next chapter we look at another reason "we know what we know" and explore another famous recitative from the appoggiatura perspective.

Are you still having fun singing your onset, *messa di voce* and portamento exercises? Additionally, exult in the appoggiaturas of Lesson 8 – Corri would be proud that you learned his lessons so well!

Lesson 8 Grammar

subject
verb
object
adjective
adverb
predicate noun, adv, or adj
prepositional phrase
interjection
conjunction
interrogative pronoun

Senza l'amabile
Dio di Citera
I dì non tornano
Di primavera ,
Non fpira un zeffiro ,
Non fpunta un fior.
L'erbe ful margine
Del fonte amico ,
Le piante vedove
Sul colle aprico
Per lui riveftono
L'antico onor.

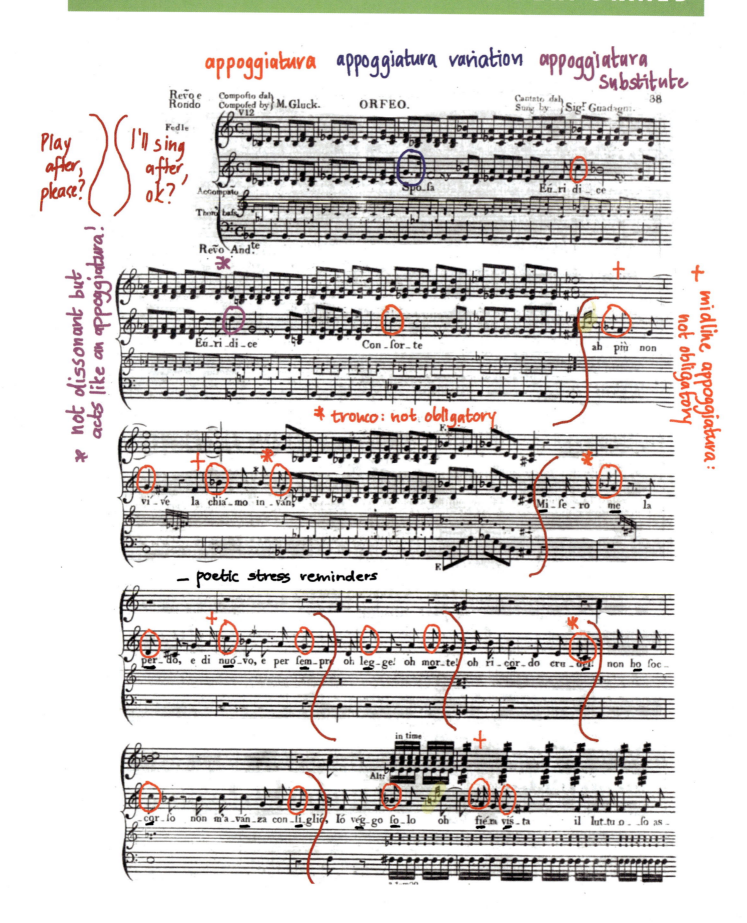

Corri, A Select Collection of the Most Admired Songs, Duetts, etc. (1779)

128

Corri, *A Select Collection of the Most Admired Songs, Duetts, etc.* (1779)

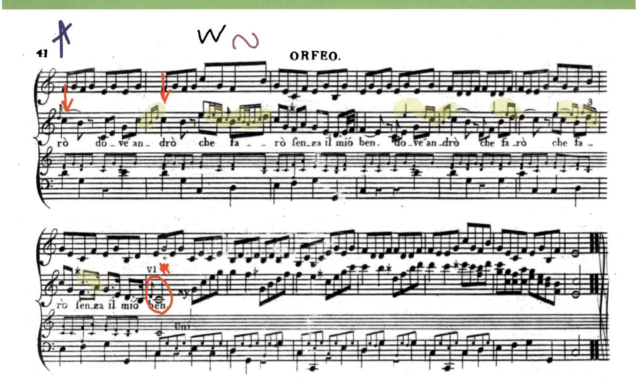

Practice Journal

_____ , 20 ___

_____

_____

_____

_____ , 20 ___

_____

_____

_____

_____ , 20 ___

_____

_____

_____

When you sing Lesson 8 today, make sure that you don't put (dynamic) accents on the appoggiaturas. Lean into them from a timing perspective (make them long) and maintain your dynamic plan through each phrase. Don't let dynamics happen to you! If you sing every appoggiatura twice as loudly as the rest of the line, people "won't like them" with good reason. They will tell you they don't like the appoggiatura, when, in fact, they don't like the way you sing them. Then you are where you don't want to be: in a battle about whether we "like" or "don't like" the appoggiatura. You can avoid this battle by singing smoothly through them.

I know the previous chapter was on the geeky side, and this one is as well. Apologies! It is a fine line we walk between just enough and too much information. In my defense I can just say that the topic of the appoggiatura STILL leads to much confusion, and I want to take the opportunity here to arm you with some solid proof when you decide how to sing your Handel, Mozart, Rossini and Donizetti. Oh, and Cimarosa!

Opinion: Cimarosa is fantastic with appoggiaturas. Without... not so much.... Only the truly great composers transcend our bleaching/filtering of dissonance out of their music – mere mortals do not survive us as valiantly.

Now let us look at an example of "another way we know what we know." On page 133-4 you see the Countess's recitative as reproduced in a "practice book."

We can infer a lot from looking at the **'Schirmer anthologies' of the past**. During the same time the Italians were writing about the Italian tradition in London (and elsewhere), they were teaching it and compiling early versions of "aria books" for their students. Luckily quite a few of them survived. They are fascinating in multiple ways: choice of arias/songs, editions (often from around the time they were in use), and handwritten notes added to the score – most often by the teacher. They provide snapshots of specific moments in history. This gives me pause: what will people think 200 years from now when they look at what we wrote in our anthologies?

A note about our study material: It is important to know as much as you can about the edition you are looking at. It is especially important to date it effectively. Failing to do so leaves one subject to disagreement about not only its authenticity, but its applicability – how close to Mozart or how far removed is it? One way we can date an edition is to research whatever details we can find on it. In this case we have the address of the printer. You see it right under "Mozart". It was printed by Goulding D'Almaine Potter & Co (20 Soho Square, London). George Goulding was reportedly in business before 1784; *Le nozze di Figaro* had its London premiere in 1789 after its premiere in Vienna in 1786. The publisher had their address at Soho Square since late 1811. At some point in the early 1830's Goulding's name is dropped from the company name. Our example thus was printed and used some time between 1811 and 1830ish. This would have been easily during Mozart's lifetime if he lived as long as Haydn. I bore you with these details since people often assume that these examples are "romanticizing Mozart."

> **While we're thinking about what happened when:**
> Consider that Mozart would have been 60 at the premiere of
> Il barbiere di Siviglia, 74 for Anna Bolena, and 75 for Norma.
> **"Style"** does not cut as easily into courses and semesters as some
> would have you believe.

Our example is of particular interest, since we see two layers of information on the appoggiatura:

1. The editor suggested appoggiaturas by printing them in small notes (in the style of Donizetti). I dare say this editor did a better job than those at Schirmer when it comes to suggesting appoggiaturas.
2. The teacher crossed out the appoggiaturas he either did not "like" or did not "require" the student to execute. Whichever it was, we don't know, but it does not matter as we will shortly see.

> **Review of the simple "when" of the appoggiatura:**
> Whenever there are two (or three) of the same pitches
> at the end of a phrase (or member of a phrase),
> we support the prosodic accent with an appoggiatura.
> **Another way of saying this:**
> Whenever you punctuate (whether you breathe or not),
> you place an appoggiatura.

You may also use the appoggiatura in the following cases, but you don't have to:

- In the middle of a line (again the purpose is to promote the prosody and give shape to the melodic line)
- If the phrase (or member of a phrase) ends in *tronco*, i.e. there is only one note because there is only one syllable

> **What to do with all the printed rests in recitative?**
> We will discuss this in more detail when we talk about recitative in Lesson 14, but here is for now a simple explanation since it comes up in our study material. **Composers were taught to place rests at the end of the poetic lines of "versi sciolti" to clarify the poetic form for the singer.** If you choose to "read across that line ending" you may ignore the rest – just like you might read across a line ending in English blank verse. Mozart reads across the line ending a couple of times in his setting already.

Here is Da Ponte's verse:

E Susanna non viene*! Sono ansiosa
Di saper come il Conte
Accolse la proposta. Alquanto ardito
Il progetto mi par; e ad uno sposo
Si vivace e geloso...
Ma che mal c'è? Cangiando i miei vestiti
Con quelli di Susanna, e i suoi co' miei...
Al favor della notte... O cielo! A quale
Umil stato fatale io son ridotta
Da un consorte crudel; che, dopo avermi,
Con un misto inaudito
D'infedeltà , di gelosie, di sdegni,
Prima amata, indi offesa, e alfin tradita,
Fammi or cercar da una mia serva aita!

*Note that Mozart set this line as
E Susanna non vien! sono ansïosa

In our example, I put **circles** around the rests denoting the *versi sciolti*, and also indicate where Mozart ignored the rule and "read across the line ending" himself. I have indicated in **red arrows** all the places where the appoggiatura MUST be placed if the singer punctuates. Should the singer choose to sing across the rest after "con quelli di Susanna," it is possible either to omit the appoggiatura or keep it. **You will see that the teacher did not cross out any of the appoggiaturas that are considered obligatory by Tosi, Corri, and García.** I have indicated in **purple arrows** all the optional appoggiaturas. The teacher crossed out the "big" printed note (by Mozart) when he wanted the singer to sing the suggested appoggiatura and he crossed out the editor's suggested appoggiatura when he wanted the

singer to sing the printed note. One of my singers once sang an appoggiatura on "O, zittre nicht, mein lieber **Sohn**" in a coaching. I said, "I don't really like the appoggiatura on **Sohn**." She smiled and said, "I do." I don't think I was ever a prouder teacher than in that moment! I had successfully taught the difference between fact and opinion: she understood the rule and exercised her right to her opinion. Remember the charming smile if you plan to do the same to a conductor! Yes, appoggiatura rules of the period we study apply in German; remember Telemann? Also English. Get your appoggiatura game on in Handel's *Messiah*! **Remember:** just like *tronco* final syllables in Italian, monosyllabic words in German and English *can* have appoggiaturas but do not require them.

Remember that Corri tells us that the convention of the appoggiatura applies to both "air and recitative." Today we just happen to be looking at a recitative.

Handel: *Messiah*

Mozart: Le nozze di Figaro

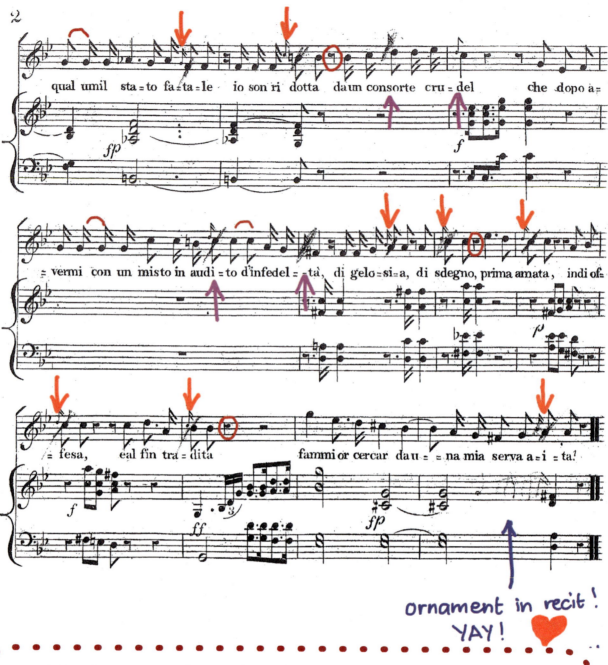

ornament in recit!
YAY!

which of my mozart and other classical arias and songs should I
revisit to make sure my appoggiaturas are on point?

Practice Journal

_____, 20 ___

_____, 20 ___

_____, 20 ___

Appoggiaturas Everywhere!

After a few days of appoggiatura research, treatises, and the general mind trick of reading one note and singing another, Derrick here chiming in! I have a penchant for finding quirky and fun things on Youtube, especially as it concerns languages and music. There is so much content out there from across the world and why not learn from it?

Ever since my high school French teacher showed us *Le Roi Lion*, I've loved movies dubbed in other languages. To fit our appoggiatura study in Vaccai, here's "Le cose che piacciono a me" from *The Sound of Music* in Italian. Why this for appoggiaturas? You'll hear that the *piano* endings are sung with ... appoggiaturas! Yes, in English, too. Listen for the primacy of the lingual rhythm that Tina Centi uses when she sings, excellent registration, a classical treatment of open and closed /e/ and /o/ vowels, and phrasal doubling: ecco le cose che**pp**iacciono a**mm**e! While the English version has the same melody, we hear in Italian more clearly just how these appoggiaturas function as appoggiaturas – leaning, lengthened, dissonant pitches. Imagine how Mozart would have notated this melody! It is translated in this gorgeous *endecasillabo* – the eleven-syllable verse that is the essence of classical Italian poetry.

Gocce di pioggia sul verde dei prati,
sciarpe di lana, guantoni felpati,
più che il sapore, il colore del tè
ecco le cose che piacciono a me!

Torte di mele, biscotti croccanti,
bianchi vapori dai treni sbuffanti,
quando ti portano a letto il caffè,
ecco le cose che piacciono a me!

Tanti vestiti a vivaci colori,
quando ricevi in regalo dei fiori,
le camicette di bianco picchè,
ecco le cose che piacciono a me!

Se son triste, infelice, e non so il perché
io penso alle cose che amo di più
e torna il seren per me!

Il miagolare che fanno i gattini,
ed il sorriso di tutti i bambini,
la cioccolata che è dentro i bignè,
ecco le cose che piacciono a me!

Un bel quaderno appena comprato,
un fazzoletto che sa di bucato,
una gallina che fa coccodè,
ecco le cose che piacciono a me!

Biondi capelli su un viso abbronzato,
pane arrostito con burro spalmato,
quando si ride ma senza un perché,
ecco le cose che piacciono a me!

Se son triste, infelice, e non so il perché
io penso alle cose che amo di più
e torna il seren per me!

Practice Journal

—————————— , 20 ——

——————————————————————————————
——————————————————————————————
——————————————————————————————
——————————————————————————————
——————————————————————————————

—————————— , 20 ——

——————————————————————————————
——————————————————————————————
——————————————————————————————
——————————————————————————————
——————————————————————————————

—————————— , 20 ——

————————————————————
————————————————————
————————————————————
————————————————————
————————————————————
————————————————————

which baroque and bel canto
arias do you sing that require
you to add appoggiaturas?

————————————————————
————————————————————
————————————————————
————————————————————
————————————————————

Lezione VIII

L'acciaccatura

*L'acciaccatura differisce dall'appoggiatura perché
non toglie né valore né l'accento alla nota.*

8th Lesson

The Acciaccatura

*The acciaccatura differs from the appoggiatura because
it does not take value or accent from the main note.*

Ben - ché di sɛn - so pri - vo, Fin

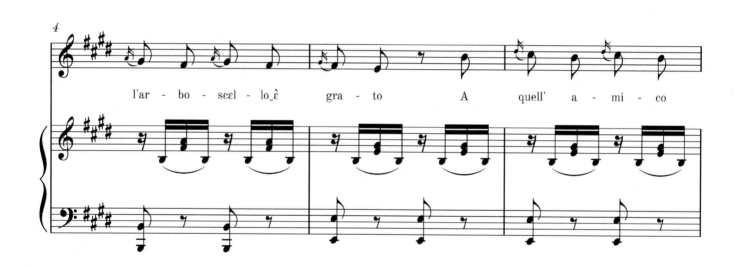

l'ar - bo - scɛl - lo è gra - to A quell' a - mi - co

ri - vo Da cui ri - ce - ve u - mor. Per

139

The Acciaccatura

The second part of Lesson 8 introduces the acciaccatura. Here starts in earnest our study of ornamentation now that we have studied in detail the mightiest ornament of all: the appoggiatura. We will explore the appoggiatura and its variations more later in the course. The most important thing to know about the acciaccatura is how to distinguish it from the appoggiatura.

> The **appoggiatura** "leans." It is a dissonant note that resolves to a consonant. It occupies **its own rhythmic space** and, since in vocal music it occurs on the prosodic accent, it is longer than its resolution.

> The **acciaccatura** is "crushed" into the note it embellishes. It occupies **the same rhythmic space as the "big" note.** It is so short that the question "does it come before or after the beat?" is unnecessary. If you do it right, whether you think of it as "on" or "before" the beat has no influence on how it sounds.

Many sources, including the main entry on acciaccatura in the *New Grove Dictionary of Music*, err in describing the acciaccatura simply as a non-harmonic note. It CAN be (and more often is in instrumental music – think of the orchestra introduction to the anvil chorus from *Il trovatore*), but in vocal music it often **embellishes the appoggiatura**, and when it does, it is by implication often a consonant note. This is true for almost all of the acciaccaturas in our lesson. By contrast the appoggiatura is ALWAYS dissonant. In truth, the pitch of the vocal acciaccatura is so short that describing it as either dissonant or consonant is a moot point. It is not experienced long enough to strike the ear as either.

The notational convention of putting a slash through the flag to distinguish an *acciaccatura* from an *appoggiatura* was not yet established consistently during the Bel Canto era. In some editions the small notes in our lesson have no slashes, but they are acciaccaturas and we know this because **we know our harmony.** They embellish appoggiaturas and **you cannot have an appoggiatura to an appoggiatura!** Make sense? You cannot lean on a consonant note to embellish a dissonant note.

Why don't you sing the lesson *without acciaccaturas* today? Can you feel how almost all of the pitches on the beat are appoggiaturas? Can you feel how the prosodic accents correspond to them? Can you feel how the prosodic appoggiatura makes the eighth notes unequal? Basically all the beats will feel just a little bit like a triplet – but not quite. Vaccai did not write the lesson in $\frac{6}{8}$ time, after all.

In the next chapter we can add the "crushed" notes and you can find places in your repertoire where you need this skill. Happy practicing!

This is Gabrielle Ritter-Ciampi singing Fiordiligi in 1924. The conductor is André Messager. By the time she recorded the other Fiordiligi aria (with recitative) around 1932 she sang it with zero appoggiaturas! This change speaks to the moment in history when the idea of "strict adherence to the score" became a dominant concept. "New music" required an increasing move towards literal reading of the score as it shook up the parameters of music: melody, harmony, and yes, rhythm.

Hopefully I have convinced you by now that legato singing was not invented by Bellini or Verdi. There is no account of someone writing: *"An amazing thing happened at the opera last night! The singer audibly connected pitches?! I had never heard such a thing before! I don't even know how to describe it exactly – it is almost as if they were carrying the pitch around! Portamento… maybe?"*

Surely someone would have written something like this describing such a revolution? No one did, because legato singing was the name of the game long before the world wants to admit. Many like their baroque and classical music "clean." Not Ritter-Ciampi. Not us.

Maybe I quote Asioli (1769-1832) here since he is a contemporary of Mozart:

Fra qualche intervallo disgiunto porterà la voce con una tale inflessione che passi per un numero indefinito di suoni di cui non si può fissare il grado.

Through some disjunct intervals [the singer] will carry the voice with such an inflection that it will pass by way of an indefinite number of sounds of which one cannot specify the pitch.

Ritter-Ciampi is clearly executing in 1924 what we can imagine to be a version of what Asioli is describing 100 years earlier around Mozart's time. No, we don't have recordings from 1800, but the world is not perfect. But people wrote - and we should read.

Lesson 8 Grammar cont'd

subject
verb
object
adjective
adverb
predicate noun, adv, or adj
prepositional phrase
interjection
conjunction
interrogative
pronoun

BENCHE' di senso privo
Fin l' arboscello è grato
A quell' amico rivo,
Da cui riceve umor :
Per lui di frondi ornato
Bella mercè gli rende
Quando dal sol difende
Il suo benefattor.

gli is an indirect object pronoun; here it represents "all'arboscello"

Practice Journal

—————————— , 20 —

——————————————————————————————
——————————————————————————————
——————————————————————————————
——————————————————————————————
——————————————————————————————

—————————— , 20 —

——————————————————————————————
——————————————————————————————
——————————————————————————————
——————————————————————————————
——————————————————————————————

—————————— , 20 —

———————————————————
———————————————————
———————————————————
———————————————————
———————————————————
———————————————————

where are the acciaccaturas
in your repertoire?
don't forget about Puccini
He loves them!

———————————————————
———————————————————
———————————————————
———————————————————
———————————————————
———————————————————

Time to "crush" those acciaccaturas onto the appoggiaturas! The important thing is to experience the "small" note and the "big" note as one event. You do not not feel the small note "sung" or "vibrated" in the same way as the main note – it is just too fast.

Our listening today is about our favorite topic: unequal eighth notes. Refer to the previous chapter for its relevance to the acciaccatura lesson. I always played Aïda/Amonasro duet from this performance to my Voice Performance class and asked them to notate the rhythm they hear in *Rivedrai le foreste imbalsamate* and onwards. Of particular interest is the fact that Toscanini is on the podium – one of the fathers of the *'come scritto'* movement. I think we can safely say that Toscanini would have passed out on the podium if he knew some people think *'come scritto'* means eighth notes should be equal!

Ri‿ve‿drai   le fo‿reste imbalsa‿ma ‿ te.   le fresche val ‿ li, i nostri templi d'ör!..

Practice Journal

—————————— , 20 —

—————————— , 20 —

—————————— , 20 —

Lezione IX

Introduzione al mordente

Il mordente è l'ornamento il più variato ed anche il più difficile, per la leggerezza con cui deve esser eseguito. Egli è composto di due, o tre note, e molto si presta alle grazie del canto senza toglier nulla alla frase, e dell'intenzione del compositore. Qui cade in acconcio il dire, che tutti quei cambiamenti che si sogliono fare nel canto (e che abusivamente sono chiamati abbellimenti), allorché sfigurano la melodia originale e l'accento primitivo dell'autore, sono fuori di luogo, difettosi e cattivi.

9ᵗʰ Lesson

Preparatory Example for the Mordent

The mordent is the most varied ornament, and also the most difficult, because of the facility and ease with which it must be executed. It is composed of two or three notes and lends grace to the singing without taking anything away from the phrase or the intent of the composer. It is pertinent to say here that all the alterations that singers often permit themselves and that are improperly called ornaments, when they obscure the original melody and the original inflection of the composer, are out of place and faulty.

La gio - ia ve - ra - ce, Per far - si pa - le - se, D'un lab - bro lo - qua - ce Bi - so - gno non ha. La

The Mordent

Next up: the mordent. For our purposes here we do not need to study the history of ornamentation in detail. Each ornament's origin, execution, and nomenclature are all aspects of what can be a lifelong study. For the purposes of our study here, a mordent is a fast(ish) **alteration between the main note and a neighboring note.** It can be written out or indicated by a symbol ᰒ . I was taught to call it "mordent" if you move through the upper neighboring tone and "inverted mordent" ᰒ when you move through the lower neighboring tone. Like many ornaments of this kind, the movement can be diatonic or chromatic. I was taught that the inverted mordent is almost ways chromatic. You?

The mordent is another **unit of pitches.** You don't have time to audiate the notes separately. If you try, you will end up "feeling stuck" or worse yet, you will insert those dreaded H's! Hear it clearly in your ear and then execute within **one breath impulse per phrase.** Just like the acciaccatura it is to be executed smoothly in the line. No random accents! I suggest you sing the skeleton first - leave out the neighbor tones.

Practicing your mordents is not only good for singing them when they are requested by the composer. Like the appoggiatura and the acciaccatura, the mordent can be used by the performer to embellish the original score. You can become a true co-composer of Mozart and the other maestros!

Caro mio ben is a gem for helping singers explore ornamentation. It is not that hard if you learn to **hug the melody**. What does that mean? You can embellish cantabile melodies by surrounding the written pitches with their neighbors (and the neighbors' neighbors!) – the **units of pitches** we are now studying in Vaccai. What I write in "Caro mio ben" is not necessarily my suggestion of how you should sing it in a performance.

This is how we practice inserting ornaments ourselves –
by starting to recognize all the places they could possibly go.

1. The bright red arrow shows the mordent exactly as we find it in the Vaccai lesson.
2. The dark red notes and symbols ᰒ ᰒ denote some places you could use mordents and inverted mordents. There are many other possibilities. I leave the third page clear for you to play with. Remember, we are just practicing skills. Put them everywhere! This will clarify for you where you like them best.
3. The blue notes are possible appoggiaturas and acciaccaturas. In the case of *ognor* on the second page, I placed an appoggiatura and then used a mordent to embellish it further. Remember how we discussed that an acciaccatura can embellish an appoggiatura? You can do the same with mordents.

We are layering our ornaments.

4. For fun, I put in mauve how this famous song would have sounded if the poet did not apocopate each poetic line. This poem is a *quinario*; review poetry and libretto chapters if you are confused.

Please don't have a heart attack because I wrote ornamentation on the first page and not at the reprise only! Slow skeletal music was often ornamented from the start. You can ornament it differently the next time or ornament it more. By skeletal, I mean the melody itself seems like a skeleton – not fleshed out – like the main structure or "bones" of a cathedral.

Now, if you are offended by ornate musical ornamentation in the baroque and classical styles, might I suggest you visit a baroque or rococo cathedral or church? Stand there, and ask yourself, "Is this too much decoration?"

Practice Journal

———————— , 20 ——

———————— , 20 ——

———————— , 20 ——

Mordents

Appoggiaturas and Acciaccaturas

English Version by
Dr. Th. Baker.

GIUSEPPE GIORDANI. (GIORDANELLO.)
(1743 - 1798.)

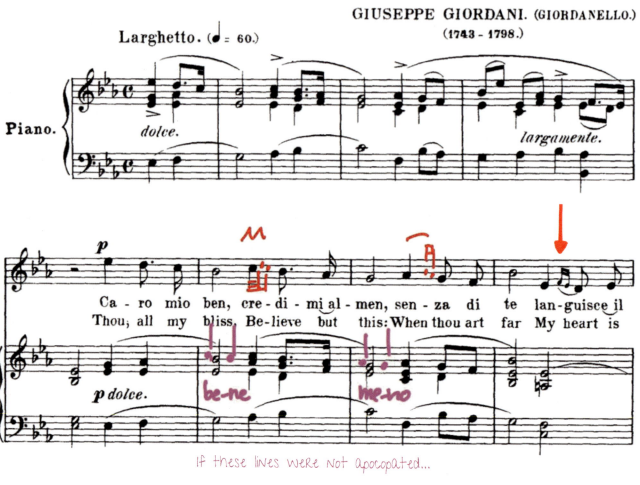

If these lines were not apocopated...

Your turn! Try your hand at writing some mordents and appoggiaturas.

If you need a break from Vaccai, why don't you sing something else and think about how working on core skills have helped you? How about singing Schubert's *Ständchen*?

This is my favorite "mordent Lied"! Here you find the movement to the neighboring note both slow in the triplets and fast in mordents. One can also call describe the patterns here as turns as we will see later. The important thing is to consider an ornament's function even if it can be called by different names.

Remember that perfectly consistent legato is the almost unattainable goal, but that should not keep you from understanding what it is and desiring it. We are half way through our work on Vaccai. It is a good time to check in with how you are doing on the mental side. Remember that **legato is not a game of perfect**. Read Rotella (*Golf Is not a Game of Perfect*) if you need reminders on how to strive for perfection while accepting imperfection.

A singer's potential depends primarily on their attitude, how well they sing, and how well they think.

Here is Heinrich Schlusnus singing *Ständchen*. The portamenti are so naturally executed – they truly connect the pitches to each other while maintaining consistent dynamic - no "droopy" or "off the voice" portamenti and no additional breath pressure either. Now, with your ear finely tuned to true legato, you will hear that Schlusnus nearly always achieves perfection. We all continue to strive for it.

The German Lied repertoire features as many half steps and whole steps as our Bel Canto repertoire does. Can you commit to singing all of them legato unless otherwise requested by the composer?

Our Schubert and Schumann really benefit from the ability to move our voices elegantly in whole steps and half steps.

Lesson 9 Grammar

subject	
verb	
object	
adjective	
adverb	
predicate noun, adv, or adj	

La gioja verace,
Per farsi palese,
D' un labbro loquace
Bisogno non ha.

prepositional phrase
interjection
conjunction
interrogative
pronoun

Practice Journal

————————— , 20 —

_____

_____

_____

_____

_____

————————— , 20 —

_____

_____

_____

_____

_____

————————— , 20 —

_____

_____

_____

_____

_____

_____

what German Lieder do you sing in which Vaccai can help you improve your legato line?

_____

_____

_____

_____

_____

Buongiorno, amici! Derrick popping in here with some review of poetic meter and libretto form. We have been safely living in *versi lirici* as we study the Vaccai lessons, yet as we inch ever closer to the recitative lesson, let's give some attention to *versi sciolti*. Keep your eyes out for the **7- and 11-syllable lines** (*settenari* and *endecasillabi*), as well as the rhyming couplet at the end. As you remember, these texts were all chosen from Metastasio operas; *L'augelletto in lacci stretto* is from *Didone*. I have marked up the original libretto as a review and did the same to a similar solo scene we all know. Make sure to review the earlier chapters on syllabification and poetic meter if something is not making sense. Some quick thoughts about both poems:

- Suffixes: learn to recognize *-etto/-etta*, *-ino/ina*, *-one*, etc. as suffixes. You'll need to look up augello, not augelletto; tortora, not tortorella, etc.

- Archaic and poetic conjugations: in Italian of this period in the imperfect indicative (habitual or ongoing past action) *credea, vedea, temea* can be what is now exclusively written as *credeva, vedeva, temeva* (third person) or *credevo, vedevo, temevo* (first person). "Ah! non credea mirarti" would now be written "Ah! non credevo mirarti"... which is an extra syllable!

Act II	**ATTO II.**
Scene 1	**SCENA I.**
Setting	
Royal apartments with a small table and chair	*Appartamenti reali con tavolino e sedie.*
Araspe, alone.	ARASPE *solo.*
Versi sciolti left-aligned	A Selene promisi — settenario (7)
	Salvar Enea, lo salverò, mi giova — endecasillabo (11)
rhyming couplet	Per ottenerla usar arte e costanza; — endecasillabo (11)
	L'ultima che si perde è la speranza. — endecasillabo (11)
Versi lirici indented	L'augelletto in lacci astretto — ottonario piano (8)
	Perchè mai cantar s'ascolta? — ottonario piano (8)
	Perchè spera un' altra volta — ottonario piano (8)
	Di tornare in libertà. — ottonario tronco (6)
	Nel conflitto sanguinoso — the same pattern repeats
	Quel guerrier perchè non geme?
	Perchè gode con la speme
	Quel riposo che non ha.

ATTO SECONDO

SCENA PRIMA.

Casa di campagna presso Parigi. Salotto terreno. Nel fondo, in faccia agli spettatori, è un camino, sopra il quale uno specchio ed un orologio, fra due porte chiuse da cristalli, che mettono ad un giardino. Al primo panno due altre porte, una di fronte all'altra. - Sedie, tavolini, qualche libro, l'occorrente per scrivere.

Character
and stage direction **Alfredo** entra in costume da caccia.

Versi sciolti
left-aligned Lunge da lei per me non v' ha diletto!... (de- *endecasillabo* (11)
Volaron già tre lune *settenario* (7) pone il fucile)
Dacchè la mia Violetta *settenario* (7)
Agi per me lasciò, dovizie, onori, *endecasillabo* (11)
E le pompose feste, *settenario* (7)
Ove agli omaggi avvezza, *settenario* (7)
Vedea schiavo ciascun di sua bellezza... *endecasillabo* (11)
Ed or contenta in questi ameni luoghi *endecasillabo* (11)
Solo esiste per me... qui presso a lei *endecasillabo* (11)
Io rinascer mi sento, *settenario* (7)

rhyming
couplet E dal soffio d' amor rigenerato *endecasillabo* (11)
Scordo ne' gaudj suoi tutto il passato. *endecasillabo* (11)
Versi lirici De' miei bollenti spiriti *settenario sdrucciolo* (8)
indented Il giovanile ardore *settenario piano* (7)
Ella temprò col placido *settenario sdrucciolo* (8)
Sorriso dell' amore ! *settenario piano* (7)
Dal dì che disse : Vivere *settenario sdrucciolo* (8)
Io voglio a te fedel, *settenario tronco* (6)
Dell' universo immemore *settenario sdrucciolo* (8)
Mi credo quasi in ciel. *settenario tronco* (6)

- Those of you who know this aria from *La traviata* well will know that Verdi changed a few of the words while, needless to say, respecting the poetic meter. This was common practice; yet the libretto of Francesco Maria Piave remained unchanged in its printed form. The above is excerpted from Ricordi's publication of the libretto for the performances of *La traviata* beginning on the first of August, 1856 in Torino, three years after its premiere.

- Note that the **subject** of the clause *vedea schiavo ciascun di sua bellezza* is **Violetta**; therefore, here *vedea = vedeva* (**she** saw)

Libretto Worksheet

SCENA II.

Figaro solo.

which verse?
ex. endecasillabo

write out the syllabification

BRavo, Signor Padrone! ora incomincio
1 2 3 4...

_____

passeggiando con foco per la camera, fregandosi le mani.

the Recit is in Versi _____

A capir il miftero... e a veder fchietto

_____

Tutto il voftro progetto: a Londra è vero?

_____

Voi Miniftro, io Corriero, e la Sufanna ...:

_____

circle the rhyming couplet

Secreta ambafciatrice: .. ..

_____

Non (farà), non farà. Figaro il dice.

_____

just making sure you recognize this is sarà, not farà

the aria is in Versi _____

Se vuol ballare,

_____

Signor Contino,

_____

Remember here to include the line ending ex. settenario piano

Il chitarrinò,

_____

Le fonerò.

_____

Se vuol venire
Ne la mia fcola
La capriola
Le infegnerò.
Saprò .... ma piano,
Meglio ogni arcano
Diffimulando
Scoprir potrò.
L' arte fchermendo,
L' arte adoprando,
Di quà pungendo,
Di là fcherzando,
Tutte le macchine
Rovefcierò.
Se vuol ballare
Signor Contino,
Il chitarrino
Le fonerò.   *parte.*

MAKE SMART CHOICES

SPECIFIC
Break down the skill set and be specific about where you need to and want to grow.

MEASURABLE
Consider making regular recordings so you can enjoy hearing your progress. Regularly enlist the help of colleagues and mentors.

ATTAINABLE
Everything that can be seen and understood is attainable. If you know where and how to grow you will realize your goals.

RELEVANT
Regularly discover how improved proficiency in the skill set unlocks your imagination in your repertoire.

TIME-BOUND
While the search for excellence is a lifelong endeavor, every step along the way can be savored and appreciated. Celebrate your small victories.

_____

_____

_____

_____

_____

_____

Practice Journal

_____ , 20 ___

_____

_____

_____

_____

_____

_____

_____ , 20 ___

_____

_____

_____

_____

_____

_____

_____ , 20 ___

_____

_____

_____

_____

_____

_____

Lezione IX
Il medesimo in diversi modi

9th Lesson
The Same Exemplified in Various Ways

Advanced Mordents

Time to tackle *L'augelletto in lacci stretto.*

Placing this lesson after the mordent and classifying it as *"il medesimo in diversi modi"* implies that the groups of notes should be sung with a "filigree attitude" and not languidly. They are combinations of mordents (upper and lower) with other chord tones mixed in to keep you humble (or drive you crazy!). Like the mordent and the acciaccatura they **live in the rhythmic space of the note they embellish** without carving out space for themselves – unlike the appoggiatura and the turn (up next) which are space hogs! Vaccai helps us to keep our audiating ear focused on the main note by inviting us to sing it without ornamentation first. I think he knew we can use all the help we can get here! During the first iterations of this course, Boot Campers asked us to print "I survived Lesson 9b" t-shirts! You are in good company if this lesson seems truly difficult. Note how this approach of Vaccai correlates with ours inviting you to define and sing the skeleton first.

It is super hard to make rules about the **text underlay** in this lesson. To be honest I've decided it is impossible after trying for many years! Yes, Vaccai ties the grace notes to the previous syllable, but, as we have discovered repeatedly, composers were not taskmasters yet when it came to details such as these. While it seems obvious (to me!) that the new syllable is placed AFTER the grace notes on the main note in places like *Di tornare*, it seems equally more natural (to me!) to change the syllable ON the grace notes already in other places, for example on *L'augelletto in lacci*, but on *stretto*, I could go either way! *Perchè mai cantar*?! I can go either way!

How about we sing it on vowels without overthinking where they change? Do what feels natural when you sing it on the text. Try it different ways. Which feels the most elegant? Sing it the way your spirit moves you. What a touching poem. Find freedom in your breath.

I enlisted help from long time mentor and collaborator Will Crutchfield. I won't bore you with the extended conversations we have had trying to figure out text underlay rules about this lesson. Finally we decided to call it a day and he made me one of his famous "mashups." These clips were recorded between 1902 and 1910.

Maybe these clips can help us learn something that is impossible to fully explain in words. These singers were clearly adept at singing grace notes effortlessly. The voice moves smoothly through the embellishments – sometimes a little slower, often super fast. The link between the audiating ear and vocal folds is SO direct. How incredible to have a technique that will execute your imagination so flawlessly!

I think we can safely say that in more recent times ornaments are often executed (and sometimes completely replaced) by "huffing and puffing." In many cases I can imagine a modern singer explode uncontrolled air in an attempt to emote what a graceful ornament used to express. As you may have noticed by now, I'm old fashioned. You might like the huffing and puffing. I'm not here to tell you what to like, but I do want to advocate for the ability to move your voice this nimbly. Who knows? You might find all the expression you ever wanted right here: on the breath, in tone, and in ornaments.

In our mash-up there are many things to admire in addition to the masterful execution of ornamental material. How about that diminuendo in *E lucevan le stelle*?! And the appoggiatura on '*derido*' in *Questa o quella* – how charming! What catches your attention?

what have you been listening to lately? what's your take on it?

_____
_____
_____
_____
_____
_____
_____
_____
_____
_____

Lesson 9 Grammar cont'd

subject
verb
object
adjective
adverb
predicate noun, adv, or adj
prepositional phrase
interjection
conjunction
interrogative pronoun

L'augelletto, in lacci ftretto,
Perche mai cantar s'afcolta?
Perche fpera un'altra volta
Di tornare in libertà.

s'ascolta is a passive form of the verb ascoltare: why is the bird heard singing?

un' altra volta is an adverbial phrase

Practice Journal

———————— , 20 —

_____

_____

_____

_____

_____

_____

———————— , 20 —

_____

_____

_____

_____

_____

_____

———————— , 20 —

_____

_____

_____

_____

_____

_____

Continue your work on *L'augelletto*. It takes quite a lot of finesse to be able to sing our current lesson well. If you feel like an additional challenge or you need a break from practicing, you can see how good you are at playing with the ornamental ideas we have studied up to now.

So far we have practiced **upper and lower neighbor tones**: appoggiatura, acciaccatura, mordent. In *L'augelletto*, Vaccai introduced the idea of adding other chord tones to the "pitch unit" resulting in the bigger intervals in the line *Perchè mai cantar*. This last idea you will not use as often in your **hug the melody** ornamentation practice. Remember: you are not writing a new melody or a descant. Keep it close! When you are more advanced you will learn how to introduce elegantly higher and lower chord tones and knit them together seamlessly with ornaments.

I played with Vaccai Lesson 1. See if you can come up with another version. Or pick another cantabile lesson. All the lessons up to Lesson 3 are great candidates for this exercise. You can also try your hand at any other cantabile piece that is not super ornamental already. *Piangerò*, *Come raggio di sol*, *Un' aura amorosa*, *Dalla sua pace* and *Ombra mai fu* all fit the bill. Our goal at this stage is not so much coming up with versions we would like to sing in performance; we are simply getting used to seeing where ornaments might go and imagining what they might be. Stick to the ornaments we have studied in Vaccai up to now. It is a good exercise to restrict the palette in order to explore how best to use each ornament. In my experience, the thing that prevents singers from improving their ornamentation skills is resisting learning how to layer them step by step. You might have fun improvising wild ornaments, but you will probably not feel comfortable taking them on stage, and with good reason! We are trying to add pitches the composer might have reasonably added himself. That is another way of saying "in the style of so-and-so." Be imaginative within the restriction of the exercise. Neighbor tones only!

As you improve your skills, you will increasingly find ornamentation the preferred way to express **repeated material**. You will step away from the flawed "sing it louder or softer because you mean it more" model. The character does not "mean it more" because the text is repeated. This is a poem – all the words are important all the time. The poet left the unimportant ones out.

The vast majority of repetition of text is the result of purely musical conventions.

A quatrain (or two) of poetry is used to set extensive musical forms. Many of these forms have repetition as a central concept, e.g. **da capo arias** and the **cavatina-cabaletta**. Repetition of musical material means repetition of text. Additionally, conventions like **sequence**, **modulation** (and other devices used in the development of musical material), and **coda** all often require text repetition. Let us challenge ourselves to approach repeated text with more sophistication than a "one-stop-shop method acting" approach. While the birth of method acting coincides with the development of recordings, it postdates the birth of the material we are singing.

A poem expressing the emotional state of the character is not real-time acting.

In real life the character is being, not doing. Time has stopped; the mind moment is explored. The director Sonja Frisell calls it "**think time**". The best thing directors can do for us in these moments is to allow the audience to experience this suspension of time. To be a quiet voyeur of the emotion – to empathize. A great ornament enhances the beauty of the composer's skeletal line and reveals the singer's musical imagination as he becomes co-composer.

Ornamentation is exploration in "think time."

We find repetition of both musical material and text in Lesson 1. Can you see how Vaccai uses sequence, harmony and musical structure to turn a six-line poem into a regular 16-bar song? **How can the basic scale be explored with neighbor tones?** After we study the turn we will do some more ornamentation exercises incorporating turns and passing tones.

PRactice JouRNal

————————— , 20 —

_____

_____

_____

_____

————————— , 20 —

_____

_____

_____

_____

————————— , 20 —

_____

_____

_____

_____

Use mordents and appoggiaturas/acciaccaturas in different combinations to ornament Vaccai's First Lesson

Advanced singers can introduce advanced mordents like we find in Lesson 9b

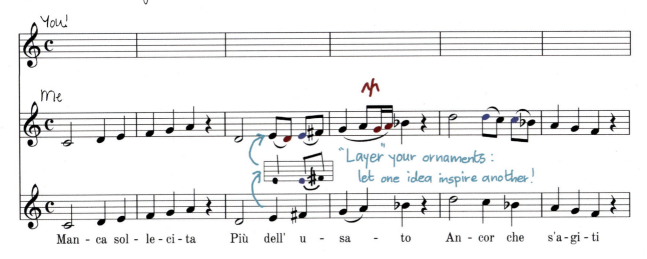

"Layer" your ornaments:
let one idea inspire another!

Man - ca sol - le - ci - ta   Più dell' u - sa - to   An - cor che s'a - gi - ti

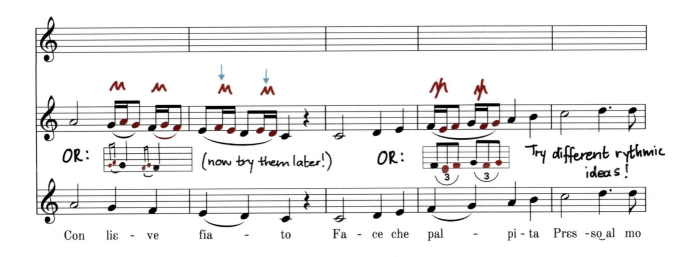

OR: (now try them later!)   OR: Try different rythmic ideas!

Con   lie - ve   fia - to   Fa - ce che pal - pi - ta   Pres - so al mo

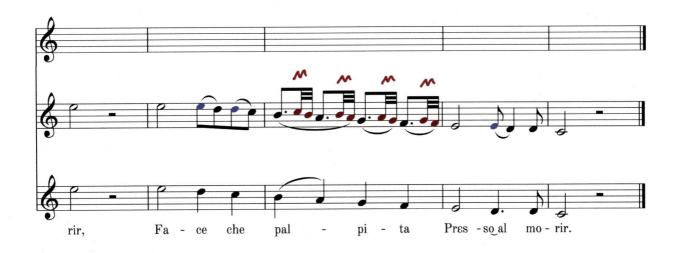

rir,   Fa - ce che pal - pi - ta   Pres - so al   mo - rir.

Lezione X

Introduzione al gruppetto

*In questo esempio si seguirà la stessa regola
indicata nella settima lezione.*

10th Lesson

Preparatory Example for the Turn

*Follow the same instructions as for Lesson 7:
Begin slowly and increase speed according to your ability.*

Quan - do_ac - cɛn - de_un no - bil _____ pɛt - to,

ɛ_in - no - cɛn - te, ɛ pu - ro_af - fɛt - to: De - bo -

lez - za a - mor non _____ ɛ. Quan - do_ac - cɛn - de_un

no - bil pɛt - to. Ɛ̀_in - no - cɛn - te_ɛ̀ pu - ro_af -

fɛt - to: De - bo - lez - za_a - mor_____ non_____ ɛ̀

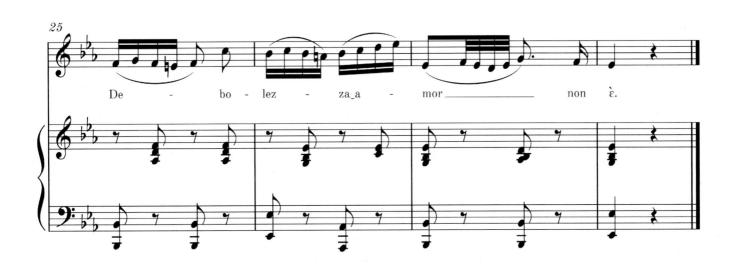

De - bo - lez - za_a - mor_____ non ɛ̀.

The Four-Note Turn

Today's lesson, while titled "Preparation for the Turn", is super important practice in itself, since the patterns we find here are strewn all over the bel canto repertoire. The turn as we find it in this lesson is very often referred to as "the four note turn."

The turn, after passing tones (Lesson 7), appoggiatura and acciaccatura (Lesson 8), and mordent (Lesson 9), is the next **unit of pitches** we study in our quest to train our voices to move nimbly and learn about ornamentation all at the same time.

As always remember that the **first step to singing fast is singing slowly**. We talked about this a lot in both chapters on Lesson 7. There is no reason to sing this lesson fast today. Heed Vaccai's instruction at the top of the lesson. Take it easy!

Remember **Two Notes** and legato tones and semitones? If you can do those, you can sing a legato turn!

A turn ∽ is constructed of five notes.

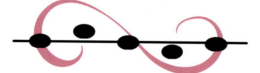

main note/upper neighbor/main note/lower neighbor/main note

An inverted turn ∽ flips the pattern.

main note/lower neighbor/main note/upper neighbor/main note
in old scores we sometimes see ∾

The four note turn omits either the first or last note of the five note turn . If the last note is omitted the four note turn starts on the consonant (pitch). On the other hand, if the first note is omitted the "unit of pitches" starts on a dissonant pitch - the upper or lower appoggiatura. You can see this clearly in our graphic.

As you sing the lesson slowly (and legato, needless to say), think about the patterns harmonically.

Is the first note of the group of sixteenths consonant or dissonant?
Does it belong to the harmony or is it an upper or lower neighbor (dissonance/appoggiatura)?

Try the exercise with the blue notes (appoggiaturas) on our practice sheet to solidify these dissonant pitches in your ear. Follow the arrows to sing the lesson as a whole.

Lean on the appoggiatura

Calling all Rosina's and Figaro's! You can employ the same exercise to clean up the coloratura in *Dunque io son*. The first part of this duet is notoriously sung sloppily. Find this pattern in your own repertoire - if you sing any coloratura, I can assure you it is there!

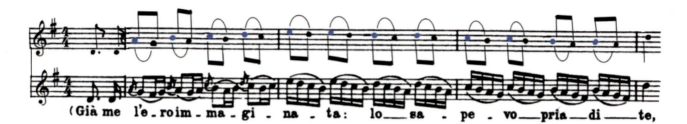

(Già me l'è ro im _ ma _ gi _ na _ ta: lo___ sa _ pe _ vo___ pria _ di ___ te,

When you sing the Vaccai lesson **with the turn** after doing the appoggiatura exercise keep your audiating ear on those dissonances. Make sure all the notes are spinning. No straight tone. Listen to Vaccai and keep it slow for now. Practice self control! I am going to repeat myself because I cannot emphasize enough how important it is:

> At any given time, you must know whether the pitch you are singing is
> **consonant** or **dissonant**

You must be able to audiate the dissonance perfectly. If your ear is confused, you can bet your bottom dollar that your voice will be too!

The four note turn is immensely useful in coloratura - it was born to run! It fits perfectly in a beat, provides movement around the skeleton and can lead just about anywhere - both from a melodic and harmonic perspective. In the next chapter we'll let it run!

> But not yet! Keep it slow. You can speed it up tomorrow.

It is amazing how many coloratura passages start with the turn. It plays well with all the other coloratura building blocks ("units of pitches") we are studying. In a later chapter we will see it in action as we examine coloratura passages from our every day repertoire.

Do you see the "little notes" on "amor **non** è and "**pet**to"? This is still a simple group of four sixteenths. Composers wrote it this way to draw the eye to the consonant note, helping you to see what I described above. You will never see this notation if the first note of the group is not a dissonance (appoggiatura). You see this same notation in the Rosina/Figaro duet in *Il barbiere di Siviglia*. All of those groups that start with the "little note" are regular groups of 4 sixteenths and they are all dissonant.

Lesson 10 Grammar

subject
verb
object
adjective
adverb
predicate noun, adv, or adj

Quando accende un nobil petto,
È innocente, è puro affetto,
Debolezza amor non è.

prepositional phrase
interjection
conjunction
interrogative
pronoun

FOUR-NOTE TURN MARKUP

Lean on the BLUE dissonant in the exercise.
Your ear needs to learn this dissonant pitch
carefully so that the coloratura will be clear.

○ CONSONANT harmony note   ∾ TURNS
○ DISSSONANT appoggiatura   ∾ INVERTED TURNS

FOUR-NOTE TURN MARKUP

IF YOU CAN HEAR IT YOU CAN SING IT!

Practice Journal

—————————— , 20 ——

_____

_____

_____

_____

_____

_____

—————————— , 20 ——

_____

_____

_____

_____

_____

_____

—————————— , 20 ——

_____

_____

_____

_____

_____

_____

"How do I vibrate each pitch when I sing fast notes?"

You don't! Remember **Two Notes** and **Intervals not Pitches**? You are not singing each note separately. If you truly execute **one breath impulse per phrase**, your vibrato cycle is consistent through the entire phrase – the pitches and the "travel time" alike. Each note does not start a new vibrato cycle. If you looked at it with the help of software like Voce Vista, you would see the vibrato cycle (of a good classically trained singer) continue between the pitches.

Remember: Portamento is the tool – Legato is the goal. Review Lesson 1 on vowels if you want to go back to legato basics.

Now spend a moment thinking about how this informs your groups of sixteenths. If you sing at ♩ = 120 you are singing fast, but not *that* fast. At 120 beats per minute you are executing 8 sixteenth notes per second. A vibrato rate of 7 complete cycles per second is fast. See where I am going with this? Even if you had a vibrato rate of 8, you would have to line up your vibrato cycle exactly with the change of pitch when singing moderately fast coloratura to achieve one cycle per note. But wait! We are singing legato coloratura — what about "the pitches" between the notes?! **This urban legend of lining up your vibrato and your coloratura will make you crazy, for sure!** Your ability to improve your legato coloratura is dependent on understanding this concept. And legato coloratura is the name of the game. The majority of singers famous for singing coloratura today are not singing legato coloratura. Please don't make me write about the "how not to." Let's just stick to "how to," shall we? You can't *do* a *don't*. Rotella writes about this as well in *Golf Is Not a Game of Perfect:*

> "One of the key attributes of the brain is that it cannot seem to understand the word DON'T. If your last thought before striking the ball is DON'T HIT IT IN THE POND, the brain is likely to react by telling your muscles to HIT IT IN THE POND. That's why it's doubly important, when facing a hazard, to focus your attention sharply on your target."

This is also a splendid reason to avoid those pesky H's! How much pitch is left after you are done with eight H's in a second?!

About vibrato rate:

Very few singers today would have a vibrato rate of 7 – a recent analysis of recordings from A-house opera singers by Will Crutchfield gave average vibrato rates ranging between 4.4 and 6.7, with an average just under 5.5. There's no disputing that vibrato rates on the whole have slowed down during the period in which we can accurately analyze. Follow this QR code to a longer discussion with Will on the topic.

See if you can sing *Quando accende un nobil petto* a little faster and put this into practice. Keep hearing your **units of pitches** before you execute them. This is how you focus your attention sharply on your target. Please **review both chapters on Lesson 7** for in depth discussion of *process versus muscle memory* and ways to practice coloratura passages. Ernestine Schumann-Heink entertains us today with the Drinking Song from Donizetti's *Lucrezia Borgia.*

where do I find the four note turn in my repertoire?

_____

_____

_____

_____

Practice Journal

_____ , 20 __

_____

_____

_____

_____ , 20 __

_____

_____

_____

_____ , 20 __

_____

_____

_____

SINGERS AND THE WORLD

Time for a little introspection on how your art intersects with the world.

Strengths	**Weaknesses**	**Opportunities**	**Threats**
What is in your wheelhouse? What do you know you know? What are you proud of?	What do you hide? What is the missing link? What do you negotiate around?	What feeds you? What are your dreams? Do you recognize opportunities when they appear?	What takes from you? What keeps you from achieving your dreams? What are you scared of?

_____ _____ _____ _____

_____ _____ _____ _____

_____ _____ _____ _____

_____ _____ _____ _____

_____ _____ _____ _____

_____ _____ _____ _____

_____ _____ _____ _____

_____ _____ _____ _____

_____ _____ _____ _____

_____ _____ _____ _____

_____ _____ _____ _____

_____ _____ _____ _____

_____ _____ _____ _____

Lezione X
Il gruppetto

10th Lesson
The Turn

The Languid Five-Note Turn

We have arrived at **Il gruppetto (The turn)** in Lesson 10. You will see that the tempo suggestion here is *Poco andante*. We often find the turn as embellishment in slow music and we'll explore using it in an upcoming ornamentation lesson.

Leopold Mozart inspires us in his *Gründliche Violinschule* to think about the turn in two different ways: an **ornament of the appoggiatura** (one note) and an **embellishment connecting two notes**. In the first case, the turn reinforces the pitch it turns around and in the second it provides connective (melodic) material between two pitches.

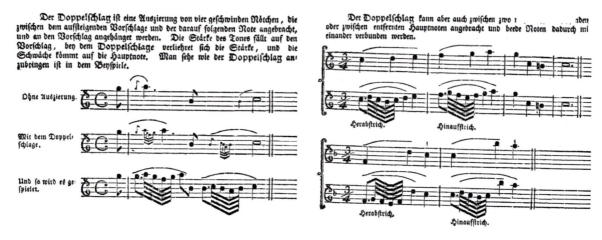

Leopold Mozart, *Gründliche Violinschule* (1756)

This approach suggests the difference between Lesson 9b and our current lesson: the mordent-like "little notes" in *L'augelletto in lacci stretto* are filigree surrounding the single pitches to which they are attached – they ornament (reinforce) that pitch. The turns in *Più non si trovano* create connective melodic material between adjoining pitches, both in small and large intervals – just like in Father Mozart's examples.

Duprez in his *L'art du chant* imagines the varied ways of executing the turn when the simplicity of notation fails us. He is referring to turns and parts of turns when he talks about "3/4/5 notes":

"Observe in the flow of this melody the different types of turn that are used: there are some which must be executed slowly and gracefully, others with vivacity, others with vigor. These are always the same three, four, or five notes and the student must apply the style appropriate to them."

While Father Mozart notates them with the same note lengths, it is important to note that composers of the time could not even conceive of something as crazy as a quintuplet! From a rhythmic perspective they picked the simplest way to notate – it never crossed their minds that singers would mathematically sing even two eighth notes equal! Much less could they imagine someone singing a dotted eighth and four sixty-fourths metronomically "correct"!

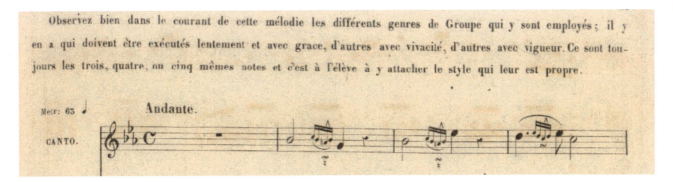

Observez bien dans le courant de cette mélodie les différents genres de Groupe qui y sont employés ; il y en a qui doivent être exécutés lentement et avec grace, d'autres avec vivacité, d'autres avec vigueur. Ce sont toujours les trois, quatre, ou cinq mêmes notes et c'est à l'élève à y attacher le style qui leur est propre.

Duprez, *L'art du chant* (1846)

Gilbert Duprez (1806-1896) was famous for singing the first tenor high C in chest in Paris. He created the role of Edgardo in Lucia di Lammermoor *and was a professor at the Paris Conservatoire.*

You can listen to different ways of executing turns in **Bel Canto Sunday Matinée Archives – As the Voice Turns.**

The character of our lesson invites us to practice our "slow and graceful" turns, so we will grab this opportunity to train our voices to execute turns full of fantasy – turns that cannot be notated exactly even if we tried! If you want to sing some of them faster, go for it! But make sure you explore the slow turn – it is the most often neglected one.

In our lesson the turn is a five note group created by the "big note" and the four "little ones" following it, connecting it to the next "big note." The most important place to keep your breath moving is **between the big note and the first little one** – that is where you create the melodic feel of the slow and graceful turn. Review your small intervals on *Two Notes*. I hope you are still doing all the Daily Exercises. I know that it takes a lot of discipline to return to the basics of barre class every day.

Once you experience the legato between the first two pitches, your breath will show you the wandering ways of the turn.

Practice your turns slowly and evenly(ish). Try not to let them create exact rhythms. You want to follow your breath and let it paint the pattern – **a limpid quintuplet** is the closest we can get to describing it. But if you try to sing an exact quintuplet you are also mistaken! You know by now that we don't do math here, right? It is easier to get the feeling in bars 7, 13, 14, 17 and 18 where the 5 notes span one quarter only. Start with these phrases. You need to bring your advanced turn game to the bars where we find the turn over a dotted quarter.

Go ahead! Paint with your imagination!

Languid turns in L'elisir d'amore

che non sa dir.

sen love ti will ra be

m'a me ra

Chiedi all'au - ra lu - sin - ghie - - ra

Donizetti, *L'elisir d'amore*

Turns on dotted notes

When the turn is placed on a dotted note and followed by another neighbor tone or other chord tone it results in a **"six note unit of pitches"**. Pinning it down becomes even harder! Look e.g. at bars 1 - 6 of our lesson. This happens in "Prendi" as well.

Follow your breath!

prendi, per me sei li - be - ro:

saggio, amoro-so o - ne - - sto.

In *Casta diva* Bellini asks the singer to move in the most limpid fashion through embellishments – technique is truly put to the test. If you pass his test, your soul flows on the breath to the listener's ear. How sad when the communication of imagination is interrupted because the singer never learned this lesson. Perfection here is impossible. It is a skill of incredible finesse. It is with good reason a star soprano must take her life in her hands and sing this kind of phrase: exposed, with the barest triplet accompaniment provided by the orchestra.

Singing is not for the faint of heart, nor the faint of soul.

By now you will hear that even Callas cannot achieve perfection. Nor will you. And it is okay. **We are human.** I'm always struck by how effective that simple statement is in explaining our flaws. As professional performing artists we find consolation in this, not joy. Our respect for the material we are bringing to life demands that we strive both to understand our flaws and to minimize them. Only then do we (and must we) cut ourselves some slack and say: **We are human.**

Lesson 10 Grammar cont'd

"si trovano" – trovarsi is a reflexive verb; therefore 'anime' are both subject and object

Piu non si trovano
Fra mille amanti
Sol due bell' anime,
Che sian costanti,
E tutti parlano
Di fedelta.

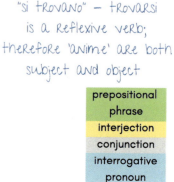

| subject |
| verb |
| object |
| adjective |
| adverb |
| predicate noun, adv, or adj |

| prepositional phrase |
| interjection |
| conjunction |
| interrogative |
| pronoun |

Practice Journal

_____ , 20 __

_____

_____

_____

_____

_____

_____ , 20 __

_____

_____

_____

_____

_____

_____ , 20 __

_____

_____

_____

_____

_____

_____

where do I find the languid five-note turn in my repertoire?

_____

_____

_____

_____

_____

Fast and Vigorous Turns

When the turn is written out in faster music we find it notated in different ways – sometimes disguising that it is a turn in the first place! The purpose of this is often to inspire **a rhythmically vigorous interpretation of the pattern.**

The bane of my existence is how the turns in *Libiamo* are butchered on a daily basis! *La traviata* is the most performed opera worldwide and I'm willing to bet *Libiamo* is sung at just about every fundraising gala - often with all the H's on all the turns. Maybe we can start a revolution here and bring legato back to this drinking song!

In *Libiamo* we find the turn written in two ways we often see notated in fast(er) music:

- Two of the five notes are written as small notes. This inspires us to sing the first three notes as a "triplet inside a bigger triplet". Is it a mordent or a turn? I say potato, you say potahto! I prefer to think of it as a turn to keep it smoothly moving on the breath. In our QR code on the next page we hear it on *sapro dividere, follia nel mondo* and *c'invita un fervido.*

(c'in) _vi _ta, c'in _ vi _ ta un

Compare this notation to Schubert's small note placement in **Ständchen**. Schubert begs the question "on the beat or before the beat" but does the audience really know what you choose? If the little notes do not occupy separate rhythmic space the question is truly moot. **Don't overthink.** It is in the vicinity of the beat and it presents as one unit of pitches. Just like in **Libiamo** this gesture becomes part of yet another pitch unit: the large note (slower) triplet, or turn if you wish. It is useful to sing the large notes first and then introduce the little ones to make sure the breath gesture stays smooth and uninterrupted. Do this with Libiamo as well!

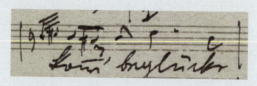

This is also how the turns in **Una voce poco fa** are written (lo sono docile). It creates the four note turn similar to the ones we practiced in **Quando accende un nobil petto** initiated with an acciaccatura. If you want you can go back to that lesson and practice all your four note turns adding an acciaccatura at the front! Keep your acciaccaturas tight/crushed and keep the sixteenths legato. Here you distinctly do NOT want to hear a quintuplet of any sort!

- An acciaccatura is introduced, crushing the upper neighbor and the main note together e.g. on *accento lusinghier* and all the other similar places. Revisit the acciaccatura chapter to keep them crushed! No leaning into them.

Here the acciaccatura IS a NON-chord tone

pp

(ac) _cen _to............. lu _ sin _ (ghier)

Io   so _ no   do _ cile

Best way to get good at fast turns is to keep practicing the slower more languid turns of *Più non si trovano*. Here is Lisette Oropesa singing Verdi's famous drinking song at Opera Philadelphia. She is one of the most consistently legato singers on the block these days. I should say that I do not approve of singers being made to stand on pianos. Why do directors make singers stand on any furniture at all?!

where are the fast, vigorous turns in my repertoire?

_____

_____

_____

_____

Practice Journal

_____ , 20 __

_____

_____

_____

_____ , 20 __

_____

_____

_____

_____ , 20 __

_____

_____

_____

Appoggiaturas in Practice

Time to return to appoggiaturas and explore how they can be varied and used as ornaments. The appoggiatura is much more than a dissonant note to support prosody. The most effective way to ornament is to introduce dissonance where previously consonance existed. Withholding the chord tone from the audience is the very best way to keep them on the edge of their seats.

The appoggiatura is the mother of all ornaments.

Other than the simple appoggiatura (one note) that Vaccai had us practice in Lesson 8, many theorists show us different ways we can support our prosodic accent. Here is **García's table of possible appoggiatura variations.**

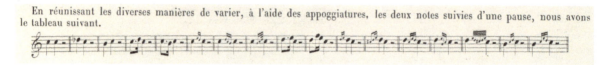

García, *Traité complet de l'art du chant* (1847)

Have a look at **Behold the Mighty Appoggiatura** on page 186. This BCBC sheet organizes García's appoggiatura variations while highlighting their resemblance to our **units of pitches** in Vaccai. Together these patterns make up our ornamentation vocabulary. Now that we have studied mordents and turns we can see how they relate to the basic appoggiatura. Why don't you try singing *Senza l'amabile* using García's suggestions to vary the basic appoggiaturas in Vaccai? I include one version. Try your own!

Ornamention is the true backbone of interpretation in the ornamental styles.

I made a version of Guglielmo's aria *Rivolgete a lui lo sguardo* using the skills we have learned. In addition to using the appoggiatura to support the prosody, I am also using it as a general ornament in *dir non sa*. Not everyone who works from the same research would say you **must** do appoggiaturas like this in *Rivolgete*. Nor do I! Some will say it is all one phrase or that it is a scale, and thus the appoggiatura is neither required nor desired. To me it is a list separated by clear punctuation and it sounds even more like a scale WITH the appoggiaturas! It is not an exact science.

Can you find the places in *Deh vieni non tardar* (both in recitative and aria) where Mozart did not notate the appoggiaturas, but you should add them? Here is Lilli Lehmann getting it right in *Ach, ich liebte* from *Die Entführung aus dem Serail*. She also does a great job explaining it in words! She notes her reaction to "modern conductors" prohibiting the classic placement of the appoggiatura. The "two masters" she refers to are Mozart and Beethoven. Masters indeed!

What would be the state of mind of these two masters if they heard to-day their wonderful recitatives that precede the arias, and the dialogue-recitatives, rendered with a total absence of the appoggiatura, that is to say, with a total loss of expression.

Every singer trained in the classical school, and to that belongs the Italian art of singing, knows and *must* know that the accent falls on the penultimate syllable of a final word, and that this accent must be brought out, not only in the spoken word but in the music. Two equal-sounding notes, on syllables that are spoken long and short, would be both a neglect of the word accent and of the musical expression, and of that neither Mozart nor Beethoven would have ever been guilty.

Up to my time no artist would have submitted to such a prohibition, and never was it suggested to me by any one of the newest conductors, because the authority of my knowledge was my protection. Does there exist, however, among the singers of to-day, one who possesses artistic influence, and who will defend himself against caprice?

Lilli Lehmann, *My Path through Life* (1914)

PRACTICE JOURNAL

———————————— , 20 —

———————————— , 20 —

———————————— , 20 —

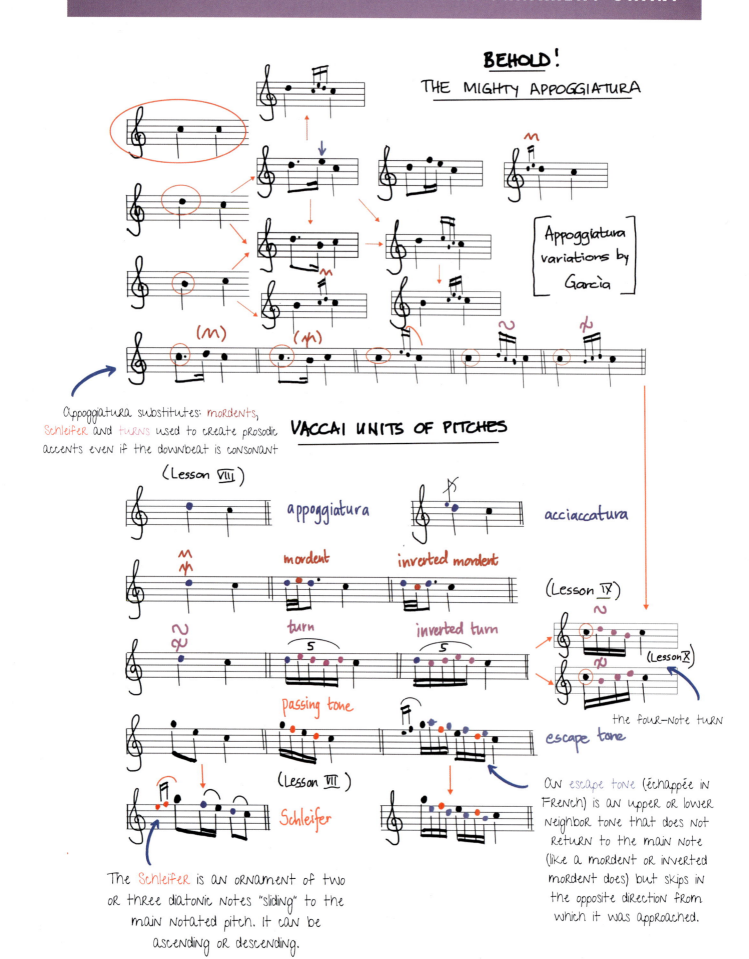

BEHOLD!
THE MIGHTY APPOGGIATURA

[Appoggiatura variations by Garcia]

Appoggiatura substitutes: mordents, Schleifer and turns used to create prosodic accents even if the downbeat is consonant

VACCAI UNITS OF PITCHES

(Lesson VIII)

appoggiatura

acciaccatura

mordent

inverted mordent

(Lesson IX)

turn

inverted turn

the four-note turn

passing tone

escape tone

(Lesson VII)

(Lesson X)

Schleifer

An escape tone (échappée in French) is an upper or lower neighbor tone that does not return to the main note (like a mordent or inverted mordent does) but skips in the opposite direction from which it was approached.

The Schleifer is an ornament of two or three diatonic notes "sliding" to the main notated pitch. It can be ascending or descending.

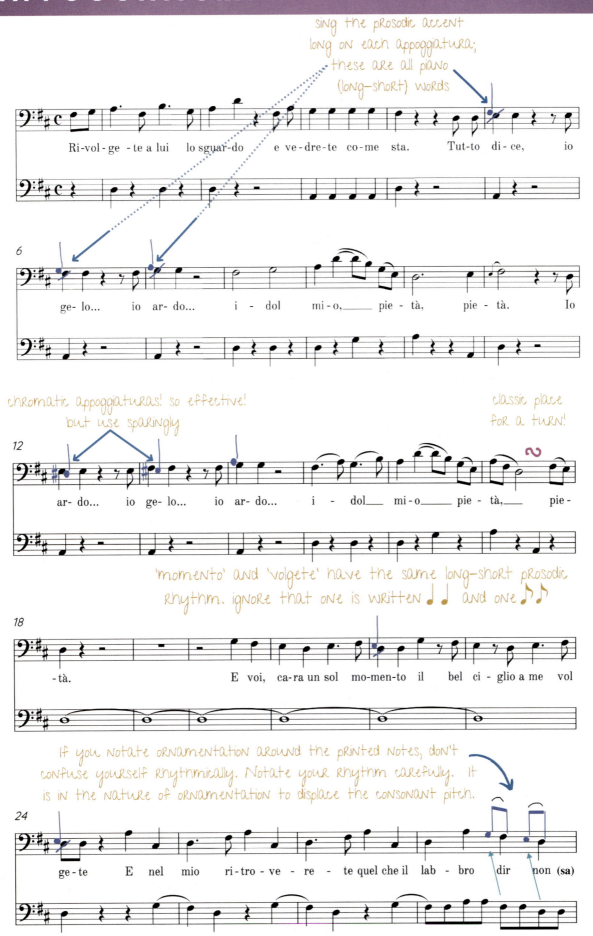

Mozart, *Così fan tutte*

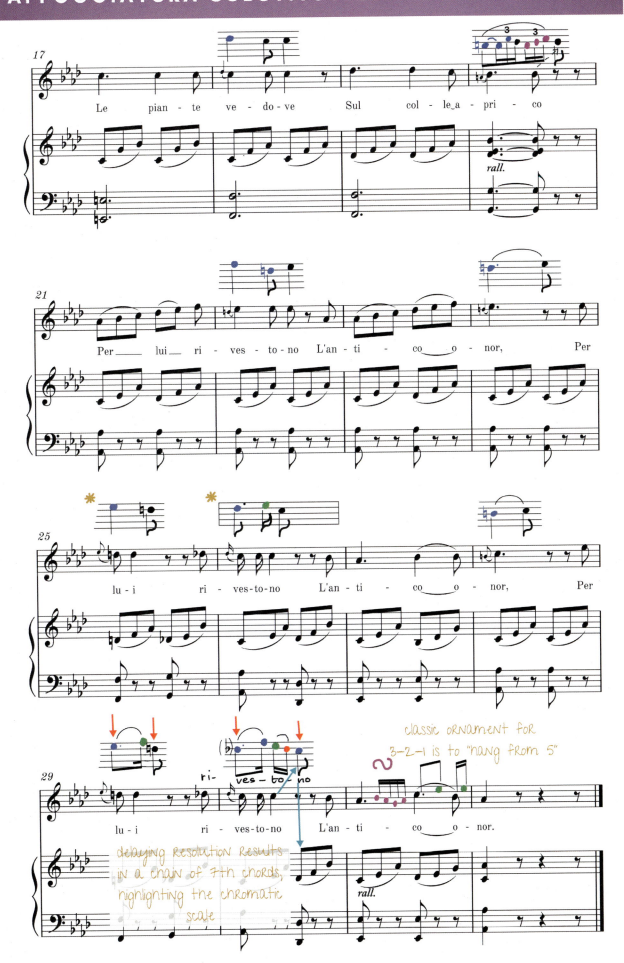

Combining Units of Pitches

Time to combine our **units of pitches** to create your own ornamentation according to your imagination and instinct. By now you have explored all the ways your voice can walk around a basic skeleton. You probably have discovered which of the ornaments your voice likes best. And you know which pleases your ear the most. Take all of this into account as you devise your own embellishments.

It brings a smile to my face how the introduction of just the simplest of ornaments makes us feel that we are collaborators with the composer. All composers of the time wrote for singers who collaborated with them in this way. How sad they would be to think that singers now are taught to pray at the altar of the written symbol leaving much of their music nakedly unadorned.

Stick to the hug-the-melody ornaments we are studying.

Try not to write pitches you cannot explain. *Are they consonant or dissonant? Is it a passing tone or an appoggiatura? Here I can use a Schleifer! This looks like a great place for a turn!*

Too many singers wander too far afield, ending up with a sheepish grin on their face when they look back and realize they have completely lost track of the thing they are trying to ornament. You know if this is true of you! Keep it close and you will feel like an ornamentation master because you will be one. These rules are not made for breaking.

The melody must still be the melody after it is imbued with all your grace and decoration.

If you don't know where to start, start by inserting passing tones and appoggiaturas and then layer your ideas from there. Here is a super simple example:

Passing tone
Appoggiatura - Acciaccatura

Mordent
Turn

Time to do it yourself! Here is *Caro mio ben,* now incorporating the turns we have studied since we previously tried our hand at this. Review Lesson 9 if needed. The Schleifer you were introduced to on our appoggiatura variation chart does not feature in Vaccai, but is a classic ornament. It turns up in *Caro mio ben.* Make your own version of *Caro mio ben* on the empty staff provided.

Maybe your *Piangerò* ornaments feel stale? Use your ornamentation tool kit to recraft them. Any slow or slowish song or aria can be ornamented like this. How does my color scheme of ornaments in *Caro mio ben* explain what Mozart was doing in Pamina's aria and what Bellini was doing in *Casta diva.*"

We will study Mozart as a master of ornamentation in an upcoming chapter. Don't turn ahead! For now you must practice the basic skills. Look at how Mozart uses units of pitches to craft ornamentation for his own aria. He wrote *Non sò d'onde viene* for Aloysia Weber in 1778 and sent these ornaments to her in 1783.

Don't be intimidated! Be inspired!

MOZART ORNAMENTING MOZART

We will discuss Mozart's use of this anticipatory notation more in Lesson 13

Note how consistently Mozart uses the appoggiatura - not only at the end of a phrase fragment, but also during it

The mordent is often used inside a scalar passage

Other harmony notes increase the scope of the melodic line

Mozart uses the turn and inverted turn right next to each other

Passing tones connect chord tones and create scalar passages

Practice Journal

_____ , 20 ___

_____

_____

_____

_____

_____

_____

_____ , 20 ___

_____

_____

_____

_____

_____

_____ , 20 ___

_____

_____

_____

_____

_____

Practice Journal

SELF-EVALUATION

WHERE YOU
WANT TO BE

WHERE YOU
ARE NOW

01. What is legato and how do you achieve it?

02. What do you listen for when you listen to other singers?

03. What are your goals for every practice, voice lesson, and coaching? Do you and your team have a solid plan to execute?

04. What do you think about when you practice? In lessons? In auditions? In the rehearsal room? In performance?

05. Where do you feel more vulnerable: in the practice room or on stage? Why?

06. What do you perceive you need to get to the next level? Is it in your control?

194

Can you name all the ornaments I used? Make sure you can name yours as well!

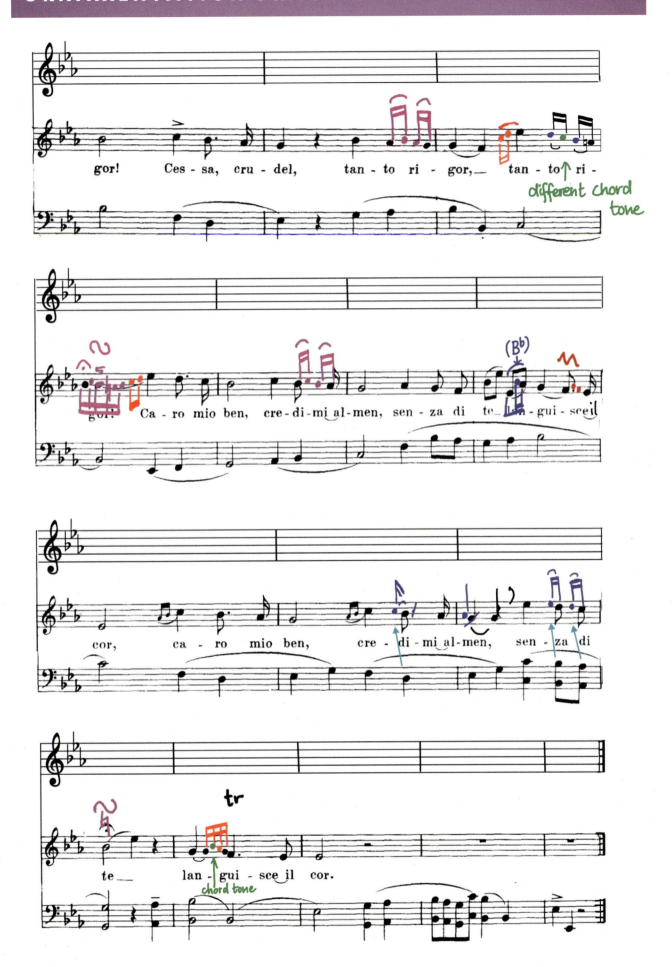

Lezione XI
Introduzione al trillo

11th Lesson
Preparatory Example for the Trill

Allegro moderato

The articulation in our score is not by Vaccai but it is essential to understanding how notation similar to our lesson was executed during this time. Refer to this example from García's **Traité** which indicates that one should "leave the note without breathing."

García, *Traité complet de l'art du chant* (1847)

Finding the Skeleton

Se povero il ruscello is one of my favorite lessons in Vaccai. In masterly fashion it brings together "repeated mordents" (harmony note and upper neighbor alternating) and turns.

Can you remember how to tell if the "little notes" in bar 16 are appoggiaturas or acciaccaturas? Look at the harmony. They are dissonances, meaning they want to lean – they both are appoggiaturas. Sing them long – even longer than their resolutions. As always, practice SLOWLY making sure those H's do not creep in. Again, I pull your attention to the fact that all of this is basically putting in practice the basic skill of Two Notes, where we started. Daily Exercises for the win!

You should be able to see the underlying structure (skeleton) of our lesson easily by now. Look at our "color version" of *Ach, ich fühl's*. See if you can do the same with *Se povero il ruscello*.

○ appoggiatura/acciaccatura

ᴍ mordent

↘ scale (passing tones)

∿ turns

In our analysis of Pamina's aria we use the same colors to notate the pitches instead of using the symbols. We add **green** to our color scheme to denote the use of **other harmony pitches** around the skeleton. Today's Ornamentation Practice invites you to partner with Mozart (and

A note about actually trilling: While this lesson requires a controlled motion between oscillating pitches, in the end the trill is an "uncontrolled" laryngeal activity. Put another way, in our lesson the larynx remains stable while singing a "sequence of mordents," while in an actual trill the larynx is "wiggling." This laryngeal motion we also experience when we sing acciaccaturas and practice yodeling for registration; the upper note is not as fully sung as the main note, meaning that it is an alteration of the main note with a lighter-function, laryngeally-tilted upper note. When this alternation is extended, it results in the trill.

The trill is an ornament of one note.
In the next chapter you can use our trill exercises to explore this in your own throat!

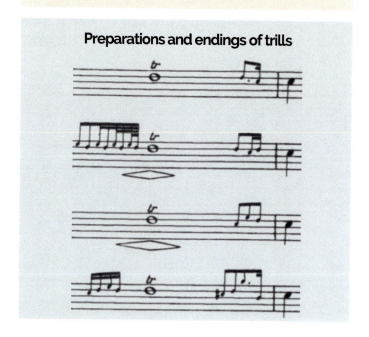

Preparations and endings of trills

García, *Traité complet de l'art du chant* (1847)

us!) by fleshing out his genius skeleton in your own original way. Stick to ornaments you can call by name. Can you see how conservatively yet imaginatively he uses **units of pitches**?

Remember: You are ornamenting THE SKELETON,
not the already ornamented version.

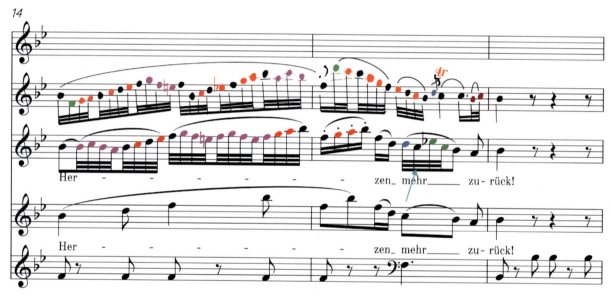

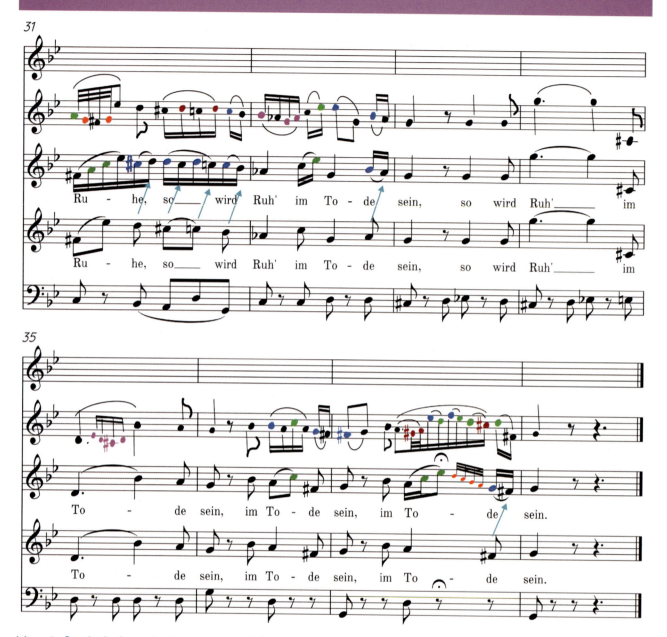

Mozart often includes coloratura passages in basically lyrical arias. He does it here in Pamina's aria and he inspires us to do it as well! He writes similar filigree like ornamental material in Andante sostenuto in **Non so d'onde viene** - the aria we quoted ornamentation examples from in our previous Ornamentation Practice. He does not shy away from 32nd notes nor the inclusion of E♭6 which is still clearly imagined in the basic cantabile spirit of the aria. Our D6 is similarly intended to be imagined as part of the fabric of the aria and not an "out of place high note"!

Lesson 11 Grammar

subject
verb
object
adjective
adverb
predicate noun, adv, or adj

prepositional phrase
interjection
conjunction
interrogative pronoun

Se povero il ruscello
Mormora lento e basso,
Un ramoscello, — un sasso
Quasi arrestar lo fa.

what arias could you write ornaments for where finding the skeleton can be tricky?

_____

_____

_____

_____

Practice Journal

_____ , 20 ___

_____

_____

_____

_____ , 20 ___

_____

_____

_____

_____ , 20 ___

_____

_____

_____

Trilling

Before we get to actually trilling, let us try to push the tempo of *Se povero il ruscello* a little – but not too fast! Keep it moderate, just like Vaccai suggests. It is very easy to let these patterns become "disconnected from resonance." We call it:

STAY IN TONE

As you sing the lesson today, consider the color scheme we use to mark up the score. We will use this system soon to explore coloratura in our repertoire. Let's clarify the reasons it is useful to look at a coloratura line in this fashion. I'm not just trying to be geeky here!

- **It helps you learn faster** since it makes sense of how the phrase is constructed. You don't just have to "learn the notes", because

YOU UNDERSTAND THE PITCHES

- **It helps you shape the line** because you must see the skeleton. You understand where the tension and resolution in the phrase exist, because

YOU UNDERSTAND THE HARMONY

- **It improves your legato** since you have been singing all these **units of pitches** smoothly in your Vaccai lessons. "Learning the notes" has become "understanding the flow" and you know you can trust yourself, because

YOUR VOICE HAS BEEN TRAINED TO EXECUTE SEAMLESSLY WHAT YOU UNDERSTAND AND AUDIATE

In the end everything comes back to allowing your breath to flow - to sing the phrase exactly how you imagine it. This is our mantra:

ONE BREATH IMPULSE PER PHRASE

Take a look at the score: I have added black to our color scheme for **escape tones.** An escape tone (*échappée* in French) is an upper or lower neighbor tone that does not return to the main note (like a mordent or inverted mordent does) but skips in the opposite direction from which it was approached. I call them **flips** when we dissect our coloratura. We find them in our lesson in bar 8. They also make a brief appearance at the end of the lesson on Turns (Lesson 10b).

Feel like doing some exercises to get you trilling?

Use Derrick's trill sheet to explore how **yodeling** and **acciaccaturas** help you achieve the laryngeal freedom you need to master the skill of trilling.

TRILLS

BCBC approaches trills as ornaments of one note and the result of motion in the larynx similar to the freedom found in a yodel and the acciaccatura.

Find flexibility in the larynx with a yodel

First on an octave, getting progressively faster

a u a u a u a

Then on a fifth

Practice dotted rhythms with upper notes

As you practice the upper dotted sixteenths, start with equal volume to the main note. Next step is to sing them slightly softer

Turn your dotted rhythms into acciaccaturas

Remember the acciaccatura does not occupy rhythmic space of its own

Widen the interval of the acciaccatura

Get to trilling!

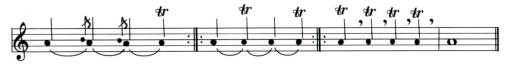

Le trille ne résulte pas de deux notes frappées l'une après l'autre et accélérées jusqu'à la plus grande vitesse, comme par exemple :

Ce passage ne sera jamais qu'un trait d'agilité qui peut précéder ou suivre le trille; c'est une variété du trille que l'on nomme *Trillo molle* lorsqu'il est placé comme il suit :

The trill does not result from two notes one after the other and accelerated to the highest speed, like for example:

This will only be an aspect of agility that can precede or follow the trill.

García, *Complete Treatise on the Art of Singing* (1847)

SE POVERO IL RUSCELLO MARKUP

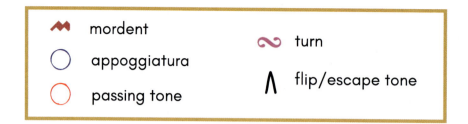

Practice Journal

_____ , 20 ___

_____

_____

_____

_____

_____

_____

_____ , 20 ___

_____

_____

_____

_____

_____

_____ , 20 ___

_____

_____

_____

_____

_____

_____

A short break from Vaccai to sing flips. "Flip" is my shorthand for consecutive thirds. Nothing gets you "off the breath" easier than a flip! To be honest I sometimes call larger "jumping intervals in coloratura" flips as well!

Any interval larger than a second can easily derail your coloratura.
Especially if it is hiding out between otherwise stepwise motion.

Ah non giunge, *La sonnambula*   Il mio tesoro, *Don Giovanni*

Here is **Come FLIP with me** to help you improve this skill. We also use these rhythms to practice any coloratura passage that might be giving you trouble. This is the same process suggested back in **Lesson 7**.

With treble voices, we often start exercises like this in the octave F4 to F5 to help clarify the "middle voice" and avoid laryngeal transitions (just to make things easier). I hate "middle voice" because it implies that there are three registers instead of two (head and chest), but I accept it to describe the octave above chest voice since that phrase is here to stay.

By now you know that this course deals with simple laryngeal registration
and leaves acoustic registration to the voice scientists!

The first pattern is consecutive thirds; the second one is where we find the **escape tone** we talked about in Lesson 11. I have no specific reason for doing them in this order – I have just always done it this way! Maybe I thought that getting people to sing ascending legato thirds is easier than descending tones and semitones? Look at me trying to figure out why I've always done something one way and not another! It seems like a pretty solid made-up reason to me. Keep this in mind when you sing the exercise:

- Our goal, as always, is **one breath impulse per phrase**. Do NOT throw your breath at the short/quick notes when they follow the dotted or tied ones. Review **Lesson 5**.
- Achieve this goal by **maintaining consistent dynamic** on the longer notes in the rhythms and carrying that dynamic through the short note to the next long note. No sausaging allowed!

MANY PEOPLE PRACTICE RHYTHMS WITH BOUNCING BREATH.
JUST DON'T DO THAT. KEEP IT SMOOTH.

In an upcoming chapter we explore more patterns you can practice in the same way. Don't turn ahead! Stick with improving your flips for now. Enjoy your practice!

COME FLIP WITH ME

Practice Journal

——————— , 20 —

_____

_____

_____

_____

_____

_____

——————— , 20 —

_____

_____

_____

_____

_____

_____

——————— , 20 —

_____

_____

_____

_____

_____

_____

Lezione XII
Le volate

12th Lesson
Roulades

Resist the urge to sing the lesson fast until you can sing it slowly and legato.
Review the Lesson 7 chapters to inspire you to train
your audiating ear to stay ahead of your voice.

Scales for Days

On to Lesson 12 we go, which basically doubles down on Lesson 7. Consider warming up with *Come il candore* today before starting *Siam navi all'onde algenti*.

ARE YOU STILL SPEAKING YOUR POEM TO START WITH?

Our lesson is a **settenario**. All poetic lines, except the final one, end in *piano*, and thus all phrases, except the final one, end with either appoggiaturas or 'appoggiatura substitutes.' Not surprisingly, the final poetic line ends in *tronco* by apocopating *mare* to *mar* to avoid the appoggiatura.

TAKE CARE TO KEEP ALL YOUR LONG SYLLABLES LONG

WHAT IS AN APPOGGIATURA SUBSTITUTE?

An "appoggiatura substitute" acts like an appoggiatura in fulfilling the same prosodic function – to support the prosodic accent on the stressed syllable/s in the poetic line.

- It can be a **different chord tone** (e.g. in our lesson on <u>venti</u> and <u>sono</u> - they feel just like <u>genti</u> and abban<u>do</u>no)
- It can also be a **different way of varying the repeated notes while maintaining downbeat consonance**. Think about "V'a<u>do</u>ro pu<u>pill</u>e." We met them in García's table of ways to vary the basic appoggiatura. Review our discussion of this when we played with different versions of the appoggiatura in Lesson 8.

Michael Spyres is a Bel Canto Boot Camp favorite. Not only he is an elegant legato singer of cantabile music, he amazes audiences (and us!) with his crystal clear and legato coloratura delivery. During the pandemic he took part in Teatro Nuovo's *Bel Canto in 30 Minutes*. His performance of our current lesson is a first rate example of truly old style coloratura singing by a singer of our day. Bravo, Michael!

Lesson 12 Grammar

subject
verb
object
adjective
adverb
predicate noun, adv, or adj

prepositional phrase
interjection
conjunction
interrogative pronoun

Siam navi all' onde algenti
Lasciate in abbandono:
Impetuosi venti
I nostri affetti sono:
Ogni diletto è scoglio:
Tutta la vita è un mar.

Try using the rhythms we sang in *Come FLIP with me* to help you keep the scales legato AND crystal clear. Do not sing fast before you can sing the lesson slowly. Sing no faster than you can keep your audiating ear ahead of your vocalising. Be inspired by some astonishing historic coloratura singing by accessing this QR code.

You can only sing what you can imagine.

Tosi is by far not the only theorist warning us against inelegant coloratura singing. But he might very well be the sassiest! *Divisions* is his terminology for coloratura.

§ 14. Let the Scholar not be suffered to sing *Divisions* with Unevenness of Time or Motion; and let him be corrected if he marks them with the Tongue, or with the Chin, or any other Grimace of the Head or Body.

§ 16. There are many Defects in the *Divisions*, which it is necessary to know, in order to avoid them; for, besides that of the Nose or the Throat, and the others already mentioned, those are likewise displeasing which are neither mark'd nor gliding; for in that Case they cannot be said to sing, but howl and roar. There are some still more ridiculous, who mark them above Measure, and with Force of Voice, thinking (for Example) to make a *Division* upon *A*, it appears as if they said *Ha, Ha, Ha,* or *Gha, Gha, Gha;* and the same upon the other Vowels. The worst Fault of all is singing them out of Tune.

Tosi, *Observations on the Florid Song* (1723)

Practice Journal

_____, 20 __

_____
_____
_____
_____
_____
_____

_____, 20 __

_____
_____
_____
_____
_____

_____, 20 __

_____
_____
_____
_____
_____
_____

My scales are going to rock in these arias and songs!

_____
_____
_____
_____
_____

Come Fly with Me inspires you to practice coloratura patterns using the **units of pitches** we have studied. The sheet differs from historical treatise exercises in a few ways:

- **It is MUCH shorter!** You will see pages packed with different patterns in the old method books. Singers take one look at them and do none of them, so I picked the ones you are most likely to encounter in repertoire.

- The exercises encompass the range of a fifth (just like the FLIP exercise page) instead of an octave. Follow the same instructions about keys and the easiest octave you find there. First sing them in the keys that cover the octave bordered by the passaggi so you can truly concentrate on agility. Expand your keys to cross the passaggi when you feel emboldened. If you prefer, you can extend the exercises to cover an octave like we often find them in the treatises.

- The patterns are inverted on the way down, while many treatises practice the same pattern ascending and descending. I do this because in repertoire we rarely come down the same way we go up. Doing the exercises this way trains your audiating ear to turn on a dime. You can double down on this idea by mixing up the bars on the sheet – **any second bar can follow any first bar.**

You can even mix the three-note and four-note exercise bars. Have fun with it!

You can use the same long note/short note(s) practice we used in the FLIP sheet. Always start slow and make sure you maintain **one breath impulse per phrase** as you work your way through the rhythms. Resist the urge to articulate with anything other than your audiating ear.

You can imagine being a violinist: the left hand's fingers move deftly with precision on the fingerboard to make the pitches clear (that is your audiating ear) while the right arm moves in a long up- or down-bow stroke (your breath). No separate bows! You can imagine playing the piano with your audiating ear while playing the theremin with your breath! Find what works for you.

Remember to enjoy your practice!

Can you see how **units of pitches** help you to deconstruct your coloratura passages? Grab your colored pencils and mark how the composer used units of pitches to craft the melismas. Keep an eye out for the turn and how often it introduces other patterns. Here are some examples to inspire you to mark up your own score!

Since you have practiced your Vaccai lessons so thoroughly, your voice will execute the **units of pitches** on command when you define them. Color-coding helps to make the eye/mind/body connection instantaneous. You can also tell yourself "turn, scale, turn, mordent, flip, scale" as you execute. You can even sing the patterns on those words!

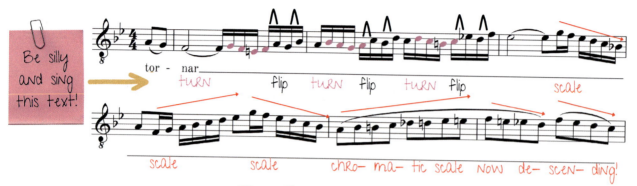

Mozart, Il mio tesoro from *Don Giovanni*

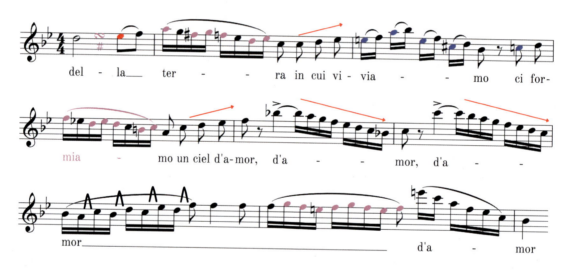

Bellini, Ah non giunge from *La sonnambula*

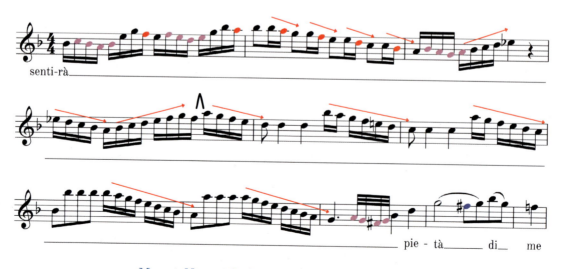

Mozart, Non mi dir from *Don Giovanni*

COME FLY WITH ME

Exercises on THREE notes

can you find and sing the skeleton?

Practice rhythms:

Exercises on FOUR notes

Practice FLIP rhythms

Then: FLY!!

when you're ready, feel free
to expand the exercise
to an octave if you want!

COME IL CANDORE VARIATIONS

**Let's try our hand at variation writing by combining
units of pitches to create a variation of Come il candore.**

Here is a quick reminder of the relationship between *ornamentation* and *variation* and how we use **units of pitches** to become become partners with the composer.

We ORNAMENT slow, melodic music – decorating an existing melody
We VARY coloratura passages – substituting patterns to fit the harmony

- We deconstruct *Come il candore* to a super basic "melody" comprising only one pitch per harmony - we could call this the **harmonic skeleton**.
- This helps us to see how Vaccai used the five-note scale which fills in the basic triad which forms **the skeleton** of his composition.
- We move beyond scales and use all the **units of pitches** we have studied to create new and extended coloratura passages.
- **Over to you!** Unlike our ornamentation exercises in which we were 'hugging the melody', we are now exploring patterns and how they connect to each other, moving through the prescribed harmonic skeleton. Keep color coding! If you can explain your patterns from a harmonic perspective you know you are winning at this exercise!

You are predominantly playing around within harmony here.

Practice Journal

_____ , 20 ___

_____

_____

_____

_____

_____

_____ , 20 ___

_____

_____

_____

_____

_____

_____ , 20 ___

_____

_____

_____

_____

_____

Bel Canto Boot Camp boasts an ever-growing roster of great mentors and collaborators.
We invited our colleague Timothy Cheung to contribute to this chapter.

Musical genres have their own musical idioms that dictate how to construct ornaments, variations, descants, runs, riffs, etc. — from jazz and blues scales to the pentatonic stylings of some popular music. Regardless of the genre, it is essential to have an understanding of harmony and how the melody interacts with it. From a practical vocal perspective, the exercises that you have been doing on **units of pitches** will provide you with a set of easily accessible tools to combine and create these vocal flourishes.

The biggest difference between the Baroque / Classical cadenza and the bel canto cadenza is the harmony above which they happen.

- In Baroque and Classical music, the vocal cadenza occurs on the I_4^6, V_4^6, or Cadential $_4^6$ (depending on what you were taught to call it), ends with a trill introducing a V^7 chord, and resolves through some version of a *Nachschlag* to the tonic.

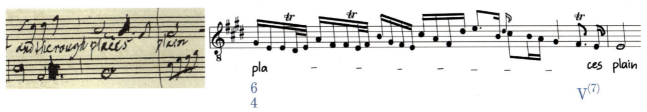

Every valley, *Messiah* – baroque cadenza by Handel written in a conducting score on the $_4^6$ chord

- As this "tail at the end of the trill" (the *Nachschlag*) becomes ever more intricate, the balance starts to shift towards the V^7 chord. We saw some of these "tails" in García's table in our chapter about trilling. A double cadenza is one in which the performer embellishes both chords somewhat equally.

Attention! Don't be lead astray by realizations erroneously skipping the $_4^6$ chord, which is often implied by the upper note of the cadential trill in your baroque repertoire. You must "find the $_4^6$ chord" by inserting the G# on "petto." Can you see how you could (not should, but something like it!) sing Handel's Messiah cadenza in Piangerò if you do this? The cadenza is not on the B major chord!

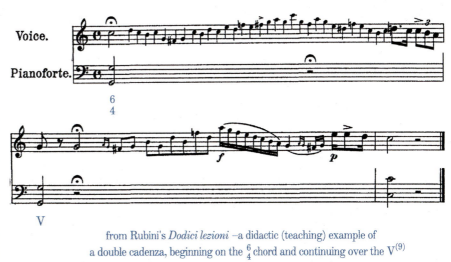

from Rubini's *Dodici lezioni* –a didactic (teaching) example of a double cadenza, beginning on the $_4^6$ chord and continuing over the $V^{(9)}$

Cadenzas present opportunities to show off your virtuosity and musical imagination. Their primary function is not to express subtext.

In the bel canto era, while we still often find double cadenzas, the cadenza mostly often occurs on the V^7 chord (and eventually the V^9 or $V\flat^9$, if you consider them to be an extension of the dominant). Opportunities for linking cadential passages may present itself in the middle of the number over other chords, so as with your ornamentation, figure out the harmonies and the chord tones so that you know what to embellish.

To shape the cadenza, it is important to **experience the dissonances and consonances over the implied harmony,** even though the accompaniment has stopped. Understand the patterns (usually in groups of four or six) and find the two-note units or appoggiaturas and their resolution to chord tones.

Baroque and Classical composers did not write out vocal cadenzas, allowing the soloist to improvise their own instead. Bel canto composers began to notate some cadenzas in their scores as examples, but they certainly expected that the singer could create their own if they wished — and usually they did. Most modern classical musicians do not improvise anymore, and it can seem like a mystifying skill. Get comfortable with the simple skill of combining different **units of pitches** to create an infinite set of possibilities!

In our examples, you will see how Rossini, Donizetti, Bellini, and Verdi crafted their cadenzas by combining various units of pitches, scales, arpeggios, leaps, etc. Remember that they were heavily influenced by an established tradition of cadenzas created by performers. By the time something was notated it had already been part of the performance tradition for some time. This is why historical classical ornamentation (e.g. the Mozart examples we have studied) will often seem like something Rossini or Donizetti might have written down!

Some miscellaneous notes:

- The early bel canto cadenzas were typically written to be sung in one breath. As soloists began to extend their flourishes, composers adapted by creating cadenzas sung in multiple breaths.
- Modulating cadenzas are usually found in the Baroque and Classical periods. (Some bel canto duet cadenzas may be more adventurous, such as the one between Gilda and the Duke.)
- You don't need to sing cadenzas on ah! Put syllables where they make sense. You can add an "Ah sì!' or "Ah no!" at the end if you want, though there is almost always a solution to be found by repeating or omitting text or pitches. Make sure that if your sentence is negated (e.g. Adina in *Prendi - "non sarai così"*) you do not sing "ah sì!" in the middle of your cadenza!
- Shape the arc of your cadenza - don't just rush to the high note and sit there!

Try to build some of your own cadenzas using the patterns you know well by now. The more you practice this skill, the better you will get at it.

ROSSINI CADENZAS

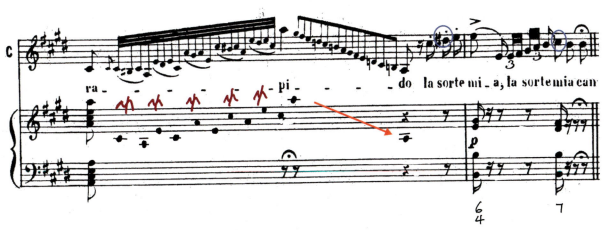

La cenerentola, Nacqui all'affanno...Non più mesta

Guillaume Tell, Asile héréditaire

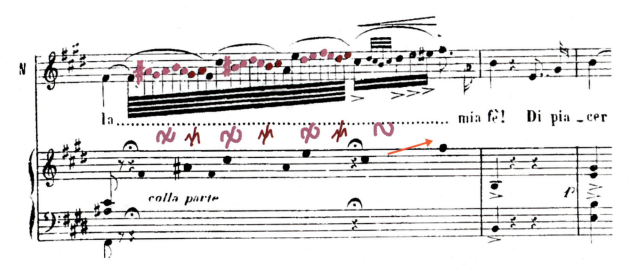

La gazza ladra, Di piacer mi balza il cor

DONIZETTI CADENZAS

Anna Bolena: Per questa fiamma indomita

L'elisir d'amore: Una furtiva lagrima

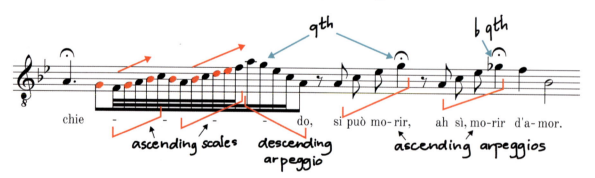

Ibid – the cadenza made famous by Caruso

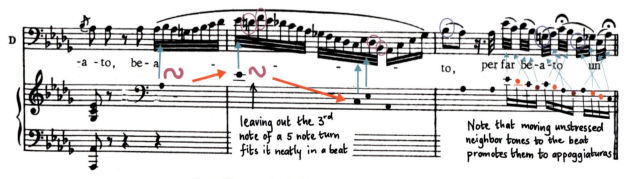

Don Pasquale: Bella siccome un angelo

BELLINI CADENZAS

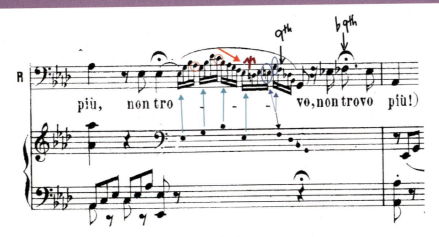

La sonnambula: Vi ravviso

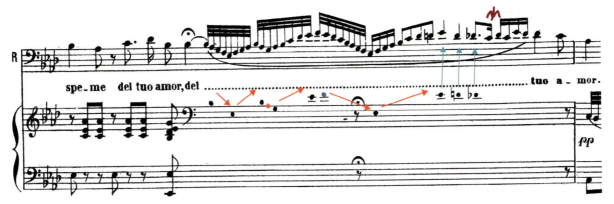

I puritani: Ah! per sempre

I Capuleti e i Montecchi: O quante volte

VERDI CADENZAS

Rigoletto: Caro nome

La traviata: È strano...Ah! fors'è lui...Follie, follie!...Sempre libera

229

list cadenzas in your repertoire and the units of pitches that comprise them

_____
_____
_____
_____
_____
_____
_____
_____
_____
_____
_____
_____

Practice Journal

_____ , 20 __

_____
_____
_____

_____ , 20 __

_____
_____
_____

_____ , 20 __

_____
_____
_____

Lezione XIII
Modo per portare la voce

Per portare la voce non devesi intendere che si debba strascinare da una nota all'altra, come abusivamente si suol fare; ma unire perfettamente un suono con l'altro. Quando si sappiano ben legare le sillabe, come si è indicato nella prima Lezione se ne imparerà più facilmente la maniera. La sola voce però di un perito maestro è quella che ne può dare una distinta idea. In due modi si può portare la voce. Il primo è anticipado quasi insensibilmente colla stessa vocale della sillaba precedente, la nota che segue, come è indicato nel primo esempio. Nelle frasi di molta grazia o di molta espressione produce un buon effetto; l'abusarne però è difetto, perché allora il canto riesce manierato, e monotono. L'altro modo, meno usato, è posticipando quasi insensibilmente la nota, e pronunciandone la sillaba con quella che si lascia; come è indicato nel secondo esempio.

13th Lesson
The Manner of Carrying the Voice

By 'carrying the voice' (Portamento) it should not be understood that one should drag from one note to the other, as poorly trained singers do; but perfectly connect one sound with the other. When one knows how to tie syllables together well, as is indicated in the first Lesson, it will be all that much easier to learn how to carry the voice between the pitches. However, only the voice of an expert teacher can give a clear idea. One can carry the voice in two ways: the first is by anticipating the following note almost imperceptibly with the vowel of the preceding syllable, as is indicated in the first example. In phrases of much elegance or much expression it produces a good effect; the abuse thereof is, however, in error, because then the singing turns out mannered and monotone. The other way, less used, is almost imperceptibly delaying the pitch, and pronouncing its syllable with the previous one, as is indicated in the second example.

cre - do al mio pen - sier, Non cre - do, non cre - do al mio pen - sier, Non cre - do, non

cre - do al mio pen - sier. Non cre - do al mio pen -

sier, Non cre - do al - mio pen - sier.

Vaccai's notation implies that all of the portamenti
are meant to be sung on vowels, much like
Mozart's "anticipatory notation" inspires us
to arrive at the new pitch on the previous vowel
before moving on to the next syllable
(see the facing page)

Portamento on Vowels

Time to slather on the portamento in Lesson 13. We focus only on *Vorrei spiegar l'affanno* at the moment - we will get to *O placido il mare* soon.

We are reviewing a skill we have spent a lot of time talking about. You are still doing **Daily Exercises: Two Notes** and you can review **Lesson 1 on Vowels** if you want to refresh your memory about our initial discussions on the topic of legato. Listen to Vaccai: don't "drag the voice from one note to the other"!

Legato is the goal – portamento is the tool.

The portamenti in this Vaccai lesson are always sung on the vowel.

Super legato, I call it! It results in a very audible, "in your face" portamento. The "little note" inspires you to arrive at the new syllable before actually singing it, creating a "new rhythm".

Vaccai's notation is one way of *writing out the portamento.* The rhythm this execution creates is often notated by Mozart to reinforce that he is imagining this kind of "super legato" expression. He either notates it as a dotted rhythm or gives the arrival of the portamento the same value as the first note. Look at these examples from *Così fan tutte* and *Die Zauberflöte.* It asks the singer to arrive at the new pitch clearly before singing the new syllable. We have marked them with brackets. This is exactly what Vaccai asks us to do by writing the "little notes" before the "big notes".

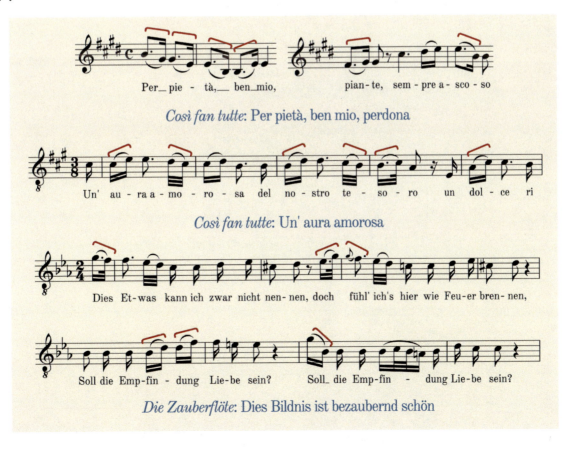

Così fan tutte: Per pietà, ben mio, perdona

Così fan tutte: Un' aura amorosa

Die Zauberflöte: Dies Bildnis ist bezaubernd schön

Remember that during **Daily Exercises: Consonants** we discussed that portamento can (and depending on the rules of diction should) happen on consonants as well? You can review Lesson 1 on Text if you want.

In the first phrase of our current lesson you would normally travel on the **rr** of "vo**rr**ei" and the portamento would be audible on the **rr**. And you would travel on the **ff** of "l'a**ff**anno" and the portamento would not be audible since you would be on an extended unvoiced consonant. Once you are ready to move on to the next chapter we will practice our lesson in this way, and we will look at a printed version of the lesson to help you achieve this. This is not to be confused with Vaccai's *Altro modo*. Hold your horses! We'll get there soon. Don't skip ahead!

For now we are **traveling on vowels.**

Do not abandon your diction though! Make sure that you still sing a double **nn** in "l'affa**nn**o" and "va**nn**o" after your portamento. (Soon we will be traveling ON those N's.)

Keep everything legato even if not notated with the "little notes." Keep the intervals on spie**gar** (bar 11) and **so** (bar 13) legato. NO H's! Also your little scale and turn in bar 15. NO H's!

Happy practicing!

Lesson 13 Grammar

subject	
verb	
object	
adjective	
adverb	
predicate noun, adv, or adj	

Vorrei spiegar l'affanno.
Nasconderlo vorrei,
E mentre i dubbi miei
Cosi crescendo vanno,
Tutto spiegar non oso,
Tutto tacer non so.
Sollecito, dubbioso,
Penso, rammento e vedo;
E agli occhi miei non credo,
Non credo al mio pensier.

prepositional phrase
interjection
conjunction
interrogative
pronoun

Look at all your Mozart songs and arias. Where do you find this "super legato" notation? Carry your voice on the breath! Sing your Mozart legato!

Practice Journal

_____ , 20 __

_____

_____

_____

_____

_____

_____ , 20 __

_____

_____

_____

_____

_____

_____ , 20 __

_____

_____

_____

_____

_____

Portamento on Consonants

Strap yourself in for a wild ride! In this chapter we explore another way to sing *Vorrei spiegar l'affanno*. Only because we know each other well by now can we attempt something this crazy - a notated "road map" of legato through consonants or as we call it

WHAT GOES WHERE

You were introduced to this idea way back in Lesson 1 when we discussed in detail the relationship between legato and language – how they work together to create the smoothly bound together bel canto line. Today we put a version of that on paper for Lesson 13. We are suggesting here how you would sing the lesson if you were not going to sing an "in-your-face-portamento" in all the intervals – review the previous chapter if necessary.

Of course it looks crazy on paper! Working on legato is a much more organic process in person. For one thing, we only discuss the intervals where the lack of legato is noticeable and impedes the flow of the musical line. But since we are not in a room together in person, and we are looking to establish a system that you can use on your own, here is a guide.

FLICK THE PITCH

Flick the Pitch is our shorthand for the "hidden portamento" – it does not pull attention to itself by either creating a new rhythm or impeding excessively on the preceding note's value. You travel quickly and efficiently between the pitches. It offers some added bonuses:

- *Flick the Pitch* helps you to **avoid unintentional scoops**. Take a look at <u>così</u> in bar 7-8. Can you see how concentrating on traveling on /o/ helps you to put the single consonant on the new pitch instead of scooping through /z/ to get there?
- Thus *Flick the Pitch* is also a great tool to **prevent erroneous double consonants** from rearing their ugly heads! Take a look at bars 16 - 18 for example: traveling quickly and efficiently on the /a/ vowel of <u>tacer</u> prevents doubling of /tʃ/ and traveling on the /e/ vowel in *sollecito* avoids unintentional doubling of /tʃ/.

Flick the Pitch also makes more sense in bar 4 (and other places) where Vaccai's "in your face portamenti" seem excessive, right? Use your dramatic and musical imagination to vary time spent in your legato connections all through the lesson. (Review p 61) Our goal is to get **one breath impulse per phrase** and **diction** to jibe together. In your repertoire you can use this system to deconstruct problematic moments – knowing **what goes where** is essential in finding a consistent way to marry legato and diction. Think of it as your **first aid kit!** Diagnose with precision where you are impeding your breath.

Many problems can be fixed by getting your legato and language in sync!

THE BCBC FIRST AID KIT

1. Sing the first note on the first vowel of the phrase. Sing it long and **establish your ONE BREATH IMPULSE PER PHRASE** while audiating the phrase as written, above your sustained first note.

2. Sing the phrase (change the pitches) on **the vowel of the first pitch**. We are going to add "hurdles" one step at a time to figure out where we impede our breath impulse.

3. Sing the phrase on **the vowels of the poem**, with consistent legato in each interval.

4. Sing the **text on the first pitch** of the phrase maintaining your breath impulse through vowels and consonants alike. Make sure the voiced consonants are vibrating freely and the unvoiced consonants are not unduly pressurized.

5. Use the guides below to figure out **what goes where**. What are you traveling on? Vowel? Consonant? Single? Double? Voiced? Unvoiced?

6. Sing the phrase **maintaining ONE BREATH IMPULSE PER PHRASE through all intervals through vowels and consonants alike**. Feeling better now?

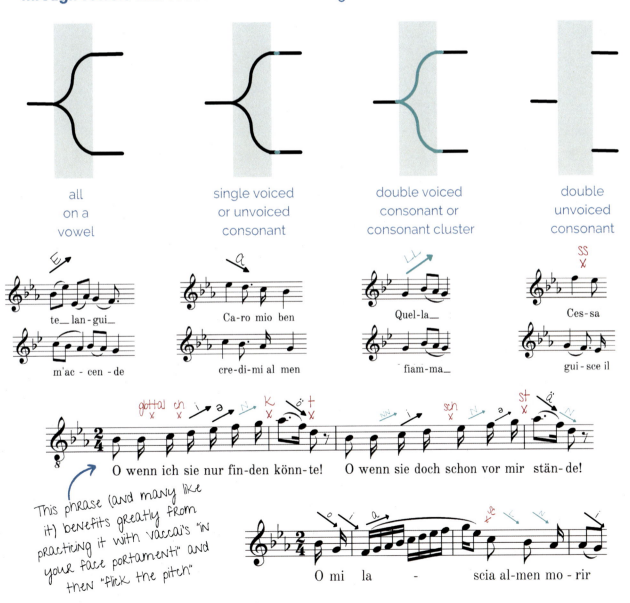

SCORE MARKUP: VORREI SPIEGAR

Refer to the BCBC First Aid Kit on the previous page and Lesson 1 on vowels for detailed explanation of legato and language.

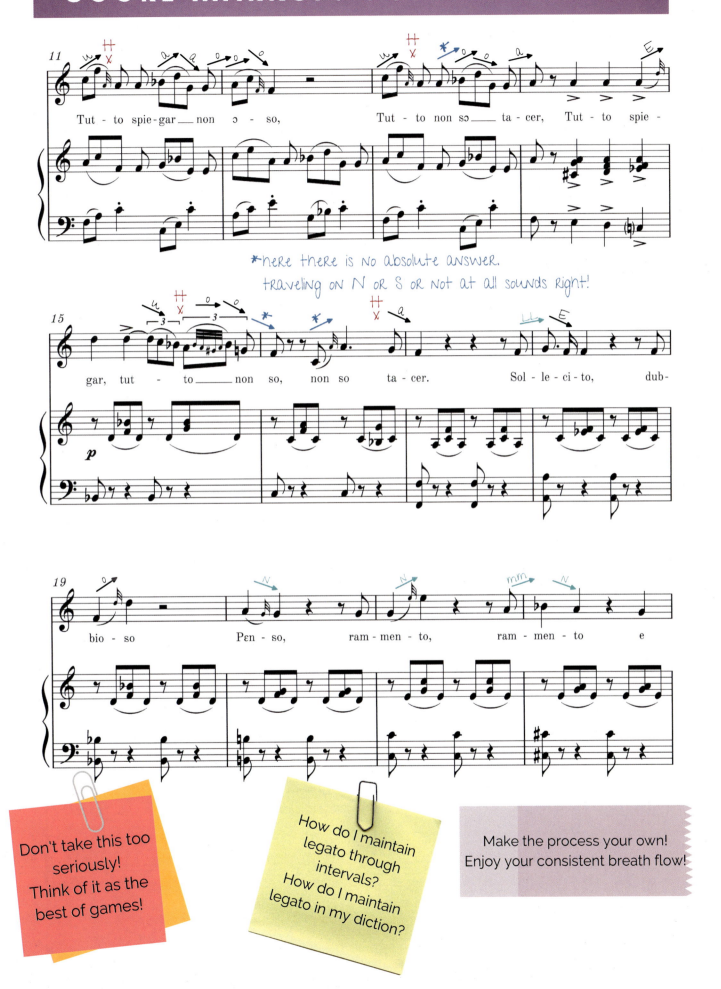

Practice Journal

——————— , 20 —

_____

_____

_____

_____

_____

_____

——————— , 20 —

_____

_____

_____

_____

_____

——————— , 20 —

_____

_____

_____

_____

_____

_____

Lezione XIII
Altro modo

13th Lesson
The Other Method

O placido il mare is "The Other Method" in Lesson 13. When I was younger I drew a line through it and wrote **OY!** on top of the page because as "the other method" of portamento, it looked like an exercise in "hooking and scooping" to me! But then I got older and learned some new lessons – it's always fun to see something in a different way, right?

In a way Vaccai's *Altro modo* is a combination of the acciaccatura and "flicking the pitch" – the fast almost imperceptible portamento. The gesture is an acciaccatura because the consonant comes at the start of the little note and the two notes happen in one rhythmic space, and it is "flicking the pitch" because the little note connects quickly to the main note.

Corri calls it the **leaping grace**
García, the **petite note inférieure**
In Vaccai it shows up as **altro modo**

> **Reminder: "What is the difference between a portamento and a scoop?"**
>
> - If you travel on the vowel and put the single consonant and new vowel on the new pitch it is a portamento.
> - If your consonant comes first and THEN you travel on the vowel of the new pitch to the new pitch, you are very much scooping!

I adopt Corri's terminology because it makes me smile, and it is way more descriptive than Vaccai's! In practice it is often used as an ornament, but it also can be found as part of the original written score.

Maybe the most famous example of the leaping grace is *Spargi d'amaro pianto* (the cabaletta of Lucia's mad scene). We also find it in Schubert's *Des Baches Wiegenlied* (the last song of *Die schöne Müllerin*). Does it show up in your repertoire? Where can you use it as an ornament? Today's mashup starts with examples of use in ornamentation and ends with old recordings of Lucia and Schubert.

Consider practicing the lesson without the leaping grace first before adding it. We are only spending one chapter here because we know you are chomping at the bit to get to recitatives!

Lesson 13 Grammar cont'd

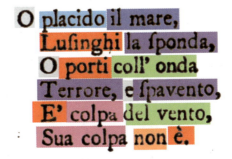

O placido il mare,
Lufinghi la fponda,
O porti coll' onda
Terrore, e fpavento,
E' colpa del vento,
Sua colpa non è.

subject
verb
object
adjective
adverb
predicate noun, adv, or adj

prepositional phrase
interjection
conjunction
interrogative
pronoun

Practice Journal

_____ , 20 __

_____

_____

_____

_____

_____

_____ , 20 __

_____

_____

_____

_____

_____

_____

_____ , 20 __

_____

_____

_____

_____

_____

_____

where do you find the leaping
grace in your repertoire?
where could you add it
as an ornament?

_____

_____

_____

_____

_____

_____

Welcome to our step-by-step guide to singing
the best Italian recitative of your life!

You are not going to see the Vaccai Recitative score for a whole three chapters!
DON'T TURN AHEAD!

Ok, you did. We forgive you, but don't do it again. Work diligently through the next chapters step by step. When you need the score, we will give it to you! This is also how you should study every recitative you ever sing. We did the same with our other lessons, and inspired you to apply that process to your songs and arias as well. *Versi sciolti* and *versi lirici* first - then the score.

PRIMA LE PAROLE, E POI LA MUSICA
First the words, and then the music

I am excited that you will be able to see how it works step by step - provided you can exercise self-discipline and not move too quickly through the material. Normally when I teach Recitative Study Techniques I am strapped for time. To be honest, whenever I coach I feel strapped for time! During a regular recitative seminar I list the steps and talk about each. People nod yes (I think they believe me), but they cannot actually see how it works. Because it does not work in one day. While the process we will be teaching here seems time consuming, it is anything but – it is truly the only way to get it right.

Now is the time to focus all your attention on libretto work with Derrick. Every singer I have ever convinced to study a big recitative role this way (think Susanna in *Le nozze di Figaro*), commented in the end that they could not believe how easily everything fell into place.

TRUST ME. IT WORKS. LET'S DO THIS!

STEP ONE: FIND THE LIBRETTO
Whenever you have a recitative to learn, either as an excerpt or as part of an operatic role, the very first thing you must do is find the libretto presented in the form the composer saw. To modern eyes, recitative may well look like prose — but think back to the ancient norm of storytelling as poetry (epic poems, *Canterbury Tales...*). Resources include:

1. Libretti d'opera – these are modern-made versions of libretti in the historical form of most of the standard repertoire operas that were composed in that style. The lifehack for this is to Google something like "la traviata librettidopera pdf" – Google will give you the PDF link without searching a website entirely in Italian. *www.librettidopera.it*
2. Google Books – find one interior line of a recitative – for example, I chose "nulla del proprio ei dona" and it gave me the Metastasio libretto of Attilio Regolo in its original form. If you're

working on Alfredo, don't Google "Lunge da lei per me non v'ha diletto" – you'll get every time it's mentioned in a book. To find that libretto, rather choose "vedea schiavo ciascun di sua bellezza."

STEP TWO: FIND THE POETIC METER

Now that you have the poetry of the recitative in its verse form (*versi sciolti*), it's time to **find the poetic rhythm/find your feet within that meter**. For now, a quick summary: recitative in this time period is composed of versi sciolti (loose/broken verse) – but loose does not mean no rules. The chief verse of Italian poetry is the endecasillabo (11 syllables). In versi sciolti we find this endecasillabo mixed with the settenario (7 syllables). To quote Baretti in *A Grammar of the Italian Language* (1778):

> Metastasio, who has brought our musical drama to its perfection, has happily mixed in his recitativos this line of seven syllables with that of eleven, without giving to it any determinate place, and simply following the direction of chance, and of his ear, which seems to me the most nice that a poet ever had.

Metastasio's verse is as follows:

PUBLIO

Pur la patria non è . . . ← *the endecasillabo continues, even across different characters' lines*

REGOLO

. . . La Patria è un tutto 11

Di cui siam parti. Al cittadino è fallo 11 ← *every new line is capitalized, but not a new sentence*

Considerar se stesso 7

Separato da lei. L'utile o il danno, 11 ← *Remember that "–le o il" is only one syllable*

Ch'ei conoscer dee solo, È ciò che giova, 11

O nuoce alla sua Patria, a cui di tutto 11

È debitor. Quando i sudori e il sangue 11

Sparge per lei, nulla del proprio ei dona; 11

Rende sol ciò che n'ebbe. Essa il produsse, 11

L'educò, lo nutrì. Con le sue leggi 11

Dagl'insulti domestici il difende, 11

Dagli esterni con l'armi. Ella gli presta 11

Nome, grado ed onor; ne premia il merto; 11

Ne vendica le offese; e, madre amante, 11

A fabbricar s'affanna 7

La sua felicità , per quanto lice 11 ← *lice–felice rhyming couplet!*

Al destin de' mortali esser felice. 11

So now that we have the poem in the correct form, **read through it slowly, but theatrically**. Remember that amplification was not in Metastasio's mind – it didn't exist! Channel your imagination of Abe Lincoln proclaiming the Gettysburg address (or your own impassioned former head of state in a pre-microphone era) as you orate the poetry of Metastasio where Regulus explains to Publius that recovering his personal liberty at the expense of his country would be guilt-worthy.

Find the feet of the poetry – the stresses will often fall on the even syllables (2 4 6 8 10), though this is variable. The lingual rhythm will hold your hand on this first trip through. Find the joy in how the words feel in your mouth. Support your speech as if you were speaking to a crowd. Remember to take time on your long syllables. This first step through the recitative is a 'tasting' of sorts where you partner with the text to make it come alive – see what jumps out at you!

Read through it again now – even if you don't speak Italian fluently, you will have some natural hunch of what words might be more important. The penultimate syllable of each poetic line is the only one which requires a true accent – and as you read on, try to **find which are the most important accents to show**. We will have more specific information later when we go through the translation steps, but to quote Baretti again:

> ....a delicate ear would soon be cloyed with such accents if they were continued throughout a whole stanza, because sameness of sounds causes a disgustful insipidity.

Sorry, I just find the bluntness of his *Introduction to the Italian Language* both charming and amusing. In the next chapter we will go over translation and diction in more detail and how they help us give shape to our recitative. No disgustful insipidity here!

This is a good time to learn some New Recitatives! List the ones you know you should learn, but have not! List the big "Recitative Roles" you need to study

_____

_____

_____

_____

_____

_____

_____

_____

248

Practice Journal

——————— , 20 —

_____

_____

_____

_____

_____

——————— , 20 —

_____

_____

_____

_____

_____

——————— , 20 —

_____

_____

_____

_____

_____

We found our libretto in the correct form and theatrically declaimed our poetry in the previous chapter. We enjoyed how the language feels and sounds, and we marveled at the technique and art of Metastasio. Now in order to give better shape to our recitative, we need to make sure we understand the translation.

STEP THREE: TRANSLATION

We are going to do this ourselves!
1. Translate every Italian word you think you know.
2. Use a dictionary and context clues to figure out all you can of the rest. Good, free, and user-friendly sources include WordReference, Wiktionary, and Treccani.
3. Phone a friend. Only sometimes can this friend be Nico Castel! Sadly Nico did not translate *Attilio Regolo*, so I'm happy to say you're on your own for the more obscure stuff.

Please, please, please. If you want to grow your own familiarity with Italian

Be willing to do the work.

Type or write with your own hands and flip through the pages
of dictionaries or search through WordReference yourself!

Nico Castel did us all a great service by presenting well-researched, well-informed translations of the standard repertoire across many languages. However, for our purposes, it is

- important to **see the recitative as poetry**, which is not how he presents it, and
- crucial to the process that you try to **make your own translation of the poetry** inasmuch as you can.

When you have finished your translation, take a look: does it read as elegantly as you would like? If not, find a way to make it more poetic.

Go through the Italian again. Where are the places where your stresses, word lengths, and pacing are now influenced by your increased familiarity with the text? How can we meaningfully connect the idea of *un tutto* and *parti*? How can we contrast *l'utile* with *il danno*? What about our treatment of a list like *nome, grado, onor*? The possibilities of nuance are nearly endless – and make sure we hear your rhyming couplet at the end.

Examine the place in the sentence where the verb comes. Armed with your translation, are you sure of the Italian syntax? Syntax (word order, basically) in Italian poetry is often a hurdle for non-advanced Italian speakers. You'll remember that Latin, the language that gave birth to Italian, functions by way of having the word ending change to show you whether it is a subject, object, or other part of the sentence. Therefore, word order is not that important, because you know who or what is the subject or the object solely based on how the noun looks. Refer back to my chapter *Syntax and Word Order in Italian Poetry*. For those who want more information, Google *synthetic vs. analytic languages*. Italian lost these cases and declinations (how nouns and adjectives change to show their function in the sentence), yet in poetry the syntax remained flexible. Therefore it is up to the reader to discern how to make the verse intelligible. *Al cittadino è fallo* could very well better be understood as *È fallo al cittadino!* And where is that subject? Hint: it's an impersonal construction – it is in error/it is a mistake.

STEP FOUR: REFINING DICTION

Now, as we read through the text again with a better sense of pacing and timing, let's draw our attention to the sounds of vowels and consonants.

Vowels: Which vowels are open and which are closed? Step one is remembering that **every vowel is "closed until proven open"** – silly, I know, but don't be guilty of saying open vowels in little words like "per me." You can use the same references like WordReference or Wiktionary to look up certain words, but you might get stuck on certain verbs. For example, when you look up *giovare* it will tell you that it is a closed /o/ – of course, because all unstressed e's and o's are closed – the tonic syllable of *giovare* is *va*. This is where I like to use the DOP – *Dizionario d'ortografia e di pronuncia* (www.dizionario.rai.it) I enter *giovare*, and it tells me *gióvo*, so I know when the o is stressed in conjugation, it remains closed. You'll want to look up *dee* as well (so, dovere); I was taught to close the tonic/stressed /e/ in this word as to distinguish it from the plural of *dea* — but you will see both are possible. (This is at the end of the video.)

Consonants: Are you really sure of all your single and double consonants? Where might there be phrasal doubling? Èffallo, ècciòccheggiova, for example. Happy declamation!

Practice Journal

———————— , 20 —

_____

_____

_____

_____

_____

———————— , 20 —

_____

_____

_____

_____

_____

———————— , 20 —

_____

_____

_____

_____

_____

Lesson 14 Grammar

REGOLO.

La patria è un tutto.
Di cui siam parti. Al cittadino è fallo
Considerar sé stesso
Separato da lei. L'utile, o il danno,
Ch'ei conoscer dee solo, è ciò che giova
O nuoce alla sua patria, a cui di tutto
È debitor. Quando i sudori e il sangue
Sparge per lei, nulla del proprio ei dona :
Rende sol ciò che n'ebbe. Essa il produsse,
L'educò, lo nudri. Con le sue leggi
Dagl'insulti domestici il difende,
Dagli esterni con l'armi. Ella gli presta
Nome, grado ed onor : ne premia il merto :
Ne vendica le offese ; e madre amante
A fabbricar s'affanna
La sua felicità, per quanto lice
Al destin de' mortali esser felice :

Legend:
- subject
- verb
- object
- adjective
- adverb
- predicate noun, adv, or adj
- prepositional phrase
- interjection
- conjunction
- interrogative pronoun

Timeline:

trapassato remoto	passato remoto	trapassato prossimo	imperfetto	passato prossimo	presente	futuro anteriore	futuro semplice
		congiuntivo	congiuntivo	congiuntivo / condizionale	imperativo / congiuntivo / condizionale		

participio / gerundio / infinito (passato prossimo)
participio / gerundio / infinito (presente)

Rende sol ciò che n'ebbe. Essa il produsse,
L'educò, lo nutrì.

. . . La Patria è un tutto
Di cui siam parti. Al cittadino è fallo
Considerar sé stesso
Separato da lei. L'utile o il danno,
Ch'ei conoscer dee solo, È ciò che giova,
O nuoce alla sua Patria, a cui di tutto
È debitor. Quando i sudori e il sangue
Sparge per lei, nulla del proprio ei dona;

Con le sue leggi
Dagl'insulti domestici il difende,
Dagli esterni con l'armi. Ella gli presta
Nome, grado ed onor; ne premia il merto;
Ne vendica le offese; e, madre amante,
A fabbricar s'affanna
La sua felicità, per quanto lice
Al destin de' mortali esser felice.

Translation Tip:

ne replaces
di _____ or da _____
(of/from something)

In this chapter we build on our familiarity with Metastasio's text, the feeling of finding the feet of the poetic meter, making a translation, and refining our pronunciation.

STEP FIVE: PACING AND DYNAMICS

Within theatrical speech we have the possibility to enrich our delivery through

VARIETY OF SPEED, VOLUME, SPOKEN PITCH

Sometimes we get excited and speak faster. Sometimes we desire ultimately to be as presentational and declamatory as possible, and will speak more slowly. Sometimes the affect of the text leads us inward or makes us want to draw our audience further into us with a supported piano dynamic. García speaks of the two types of recitative as sung or spoken, and according to his examples, these are what most of us would respectively call *accompagnato* or *secco*.

Let me caution you against the idea that there is a recitative that is to be "spoken" in the modern idea of "off the voice" or fast.

As re-enactors of these characters and their stories, we must embody their speech and transmit it through the theatrical medium. While I personally might call certain recitative more conversational and certain other more presentational, **none of it is to be so rushed through or so unsung as to rob its meaning.**

Equipped with your knowledge, speak the recitative and decide – is this person speaking in a grand manner? Then it is more likely presentational and likely to start slowly. Work your way through the recitative. Where would you speed up? Where would you slow down? Where would you want to raise or lower the dynamic?

As you study recitative from roles where you share a scene with other characters, make sure you **understand the mood and tone** of what they are saying and how it compares or contrasts to yours. It is all too easy for two characters to sound like they are in the same mood/emotion once pitch gets added, even if they have opposite emotions from each other in the context of the scene.

You know where the line endings are in the *versi sciolti*. When you look at the musical setting later, you will see how the rests in the vocal line will only sometimes coincide with the choices you've made guided by the poetry.

Choose where you want to break and punctuate and where you want to elide.

Remember that commas don't necessitate stops in sound — you can use your imagination to elongate syllables, eliding over the comma but honoring that there is time to be taken. Be playful. There has to be a part of us that plays with language like a kid in a sandbox. Whatever metaphorical sandcastle you build with your declamation has to be recreated every time! Be willing to take risks informed by your knowledge and see what works.

STEP SIX: MEMORIZE

Memorize your text of recitative before looking at the pitches if you can. If you're preparing an opera role, before you go to step 3 and 4 of translation, make sure you DO open the score to make sure that the composer didn't alter the libretto. This happens every now and again, and it would defeat our purpose to memorize wrong text.

There are many devices for memory. I would strongly beg of you NOT to start speaking in unsupported tone while memorizing. Either go through silently and imagine saying the words, or speak with supported, gorgeous tone. I like to visualize the things I'm talking about while I memorize. Others like to write the text down repeatedly. Some people make hand signals! Have fun with this.

And, with no further ado, but with great fanfare: our mashup from a previous Vaccai session!

Practice Journal

—————— , 20 —

_____

_____

_____

_____

_____

—————— , 20 —

_____

_____

_____

_____

_____

—————— , 20 —

_____

_____

_____

_____

_____

Lezione XIV
Il recitativo

*Nel recitativo è neccessaria una sillabazione distinta
e decisa, e senza una perfetta accentuazione non se ne
potrà ottenere un buon effetto. Allorché s'incontrano due
note simili nel finire di un periodo, o anche più note
simili nel mezzo, quella ove cade l'accento della parola
dev'essere intieramente convertita in appoggiatura della
seguente: il che per più chiarezza viene indicato con una
a sopra la nota dell'accento.*

14th Lesson
Recitative

*In recitative a clear and confident delivery of
each syllable is necessary; and without the perfect
emphases the right effect is impossible to obtain.
When two equal notes occur at the end of a period
(phrase), or many of the same note occur in the middle
of the phrase, the pitch of the accented syllable must be
changed into an appoggiatura.*

La Pa-tria è un tut-to di cui siam par-ti, Al cit-ta-di-no è

fal - lo con - si - de - rar se stes - so se-pa-ra-to da Lɛ - i.

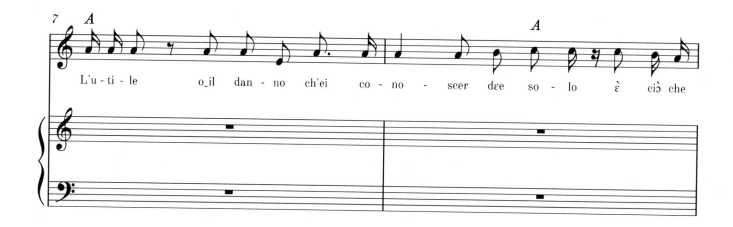

L'u - ti - le o il dan - no ch'ei co - no - scer dɛɛ so - lo è ciò che

gio - va   o nuɔ-ce_al-la sua   pa-tria   a cui di tut-to_ɛ̀ de-bi - tor.

Quan-do_i su-do-ri   e_il   san - gue   spar - ge   per   lɛ - i,   nul-la del prɔ-prio   ei

do - na,   rɛn-de sol ciò che n'ɛb-be.   Es - sa_il pro -

dus- se, l'e - du - cò, lo nu - drì: con le sue leg-gi da-gl'in-sul-ti do-

mɛ - sti - ci_il di - fɛn - de, da - gli_e-stɛr - ni con

l'ar - mi. El - la gli prɛ - sta no - me, gra - do ed o-

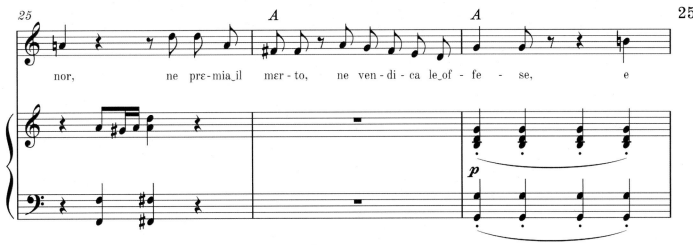

nor,   ne prɛ-mia_il mɛr-to,   ne ven-di-ca le_of-fe - se,   e

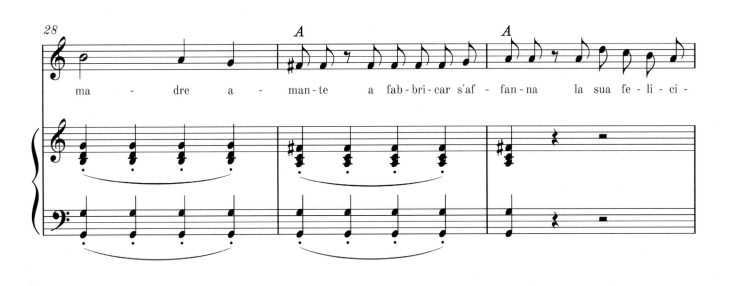

ma - dre a - man-te   a fab-bri-car s'af-fan-na   la sua fe-li-ci-

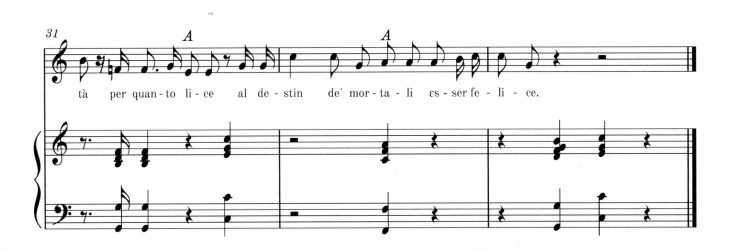

tà   per quan-to li-ce   al de-stin de' mor-ta-li ɛs-ser fe-li-ce.

Recitative: From Speaking to Singing

Here you go! Finally you can look at the marked up score of Lesson 14. It has a LOT of information on it. Here is a quick and dirty summary of the steps after your libretto study when you open the score. The steps are exhaustive. You can skip steps if they are truly second nature to you – but guard against declaring something second nature too soon!

1. **Circle the rests that correspond with the** *versi sciolti* **line endings.** Mark where the composer 'read across a line ending.' You want to be able to continue to see your poetic form in the score. (We did this way back in *Score Markup: Countess Recitative* already.)

2. **Put a line under any long syllable you might be tempted to forget** - under *all the long syllables* if you are new to recitative singing or Italian is not your strong suit. This is particularly important when you see a note value notated that might throw you off course. We have studied these conventions earlier in the course. Remember you are trying NOT to see the flags unless they show you specific information – and then they tend to show the natural scanning of the poem in any case. In our score you will see that we did away with those pesky flags that lead you astray. ○ denotes a stressed (long) syllable and ● denotes an unstressed (short) syllable.

3. **Transfer any diction notes you might have made in your libretto including phrasal doubling.** Indicate double consonants you tend to forget and draw a line through the single ones you might be tempted to double.

4. **If it is an** *accompagnato*, **plan where you need to "conduct" the orchestra** with your penultimate long syllable. You lead the "downbeat" (next stressed syllable) by singing the penultimate long syllable as an "upbeat". Remember that music of this era was not written to be conducted. You are in charge!

5. **If you are a pianist or conductor, note conventions like final short quarters and articulations** that do not come naturally to you yet. Indicate all the places you can give the voice freedom by placing the chord/s or starting the melodic interjection after the voice finishes. Likewise the singer will sing after the orchestra (piano) whenever possible. García insists we give each other space! *(All the performance conventions for orchestra cannot be covered in this course, but find on the next page the basics of timing in recitativo.)*

6. **Mark all places that require an appoggiatura** based on where you decided to punctuate when you spoke the libretto. Note places where the composer might be prompting you to change your mind because of chord placement/harmonic progress. Indicate places where you want to continue across a rest.

7. **Speak your recitative while looking at the score.** Mark any mid-line (not obligatory) appoggiaturas that might jump out at you. You might find more (or decide to take some out) when you sing. Pay special attention to the pacing of your rhyming couplet at the end of your recitative.

In recitativo accompagnato , the voice must remain completely clear
from the accompaniment, with the exception of moments of Arioso.
The chords are only played once the singing has stopped, and vice versa.

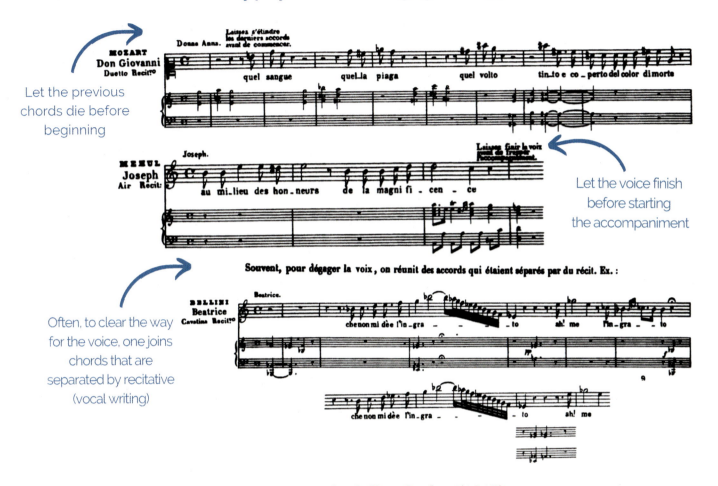

Let the previous chords die before beginning

Let the voice finish before starting the accompaniment

Often, to clear the way for the voice, one joins chords that are separated by recitative (vocal writing)

García, *Traité complet de l'art du chant* (1847)

8. **Play the chords on the piano while speaking the recitative.** Pay attention to dynamic markings in the orchestra if it is an *accompagnato*. If there are places without dynamic makings make sure to deliver your line in a way that inspires the orchestra to choose a suitable dynamic.

9. **Sing the recitative while playing the chords.** Sing it just the way you speak it – with all the nuance you developed in your libretto steps. *Try not to plunk out the notes of the recitative itself.* They are easy! If the poem falls out of your mouth easily you'll be able to sight read it even if you are not a good sight reader. Trust me: it only goes so many ways! NEVER singing your recitative (or anything else for that matter) without expression is a good goal to strive for.

YOU DID IT!
BRAVI TUTTI!

SCORE MARKUP: VACCAI RECITATIVE

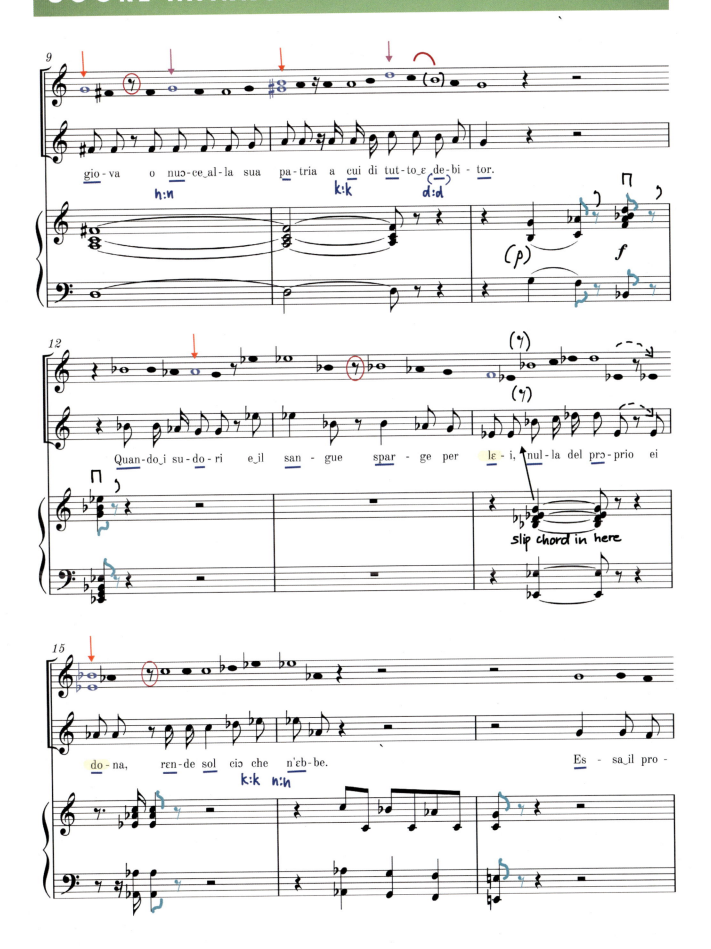

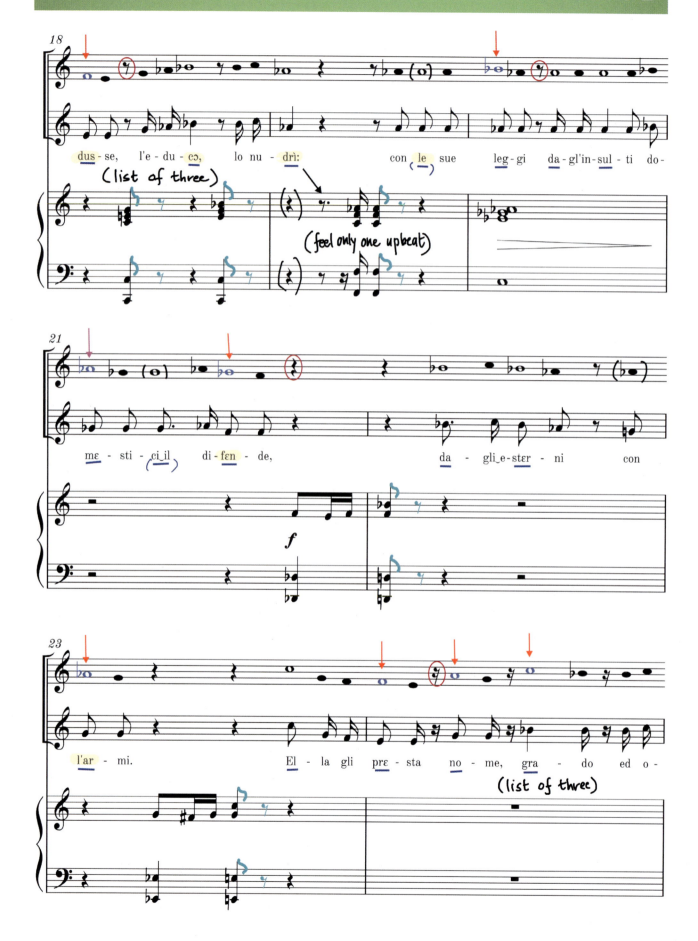

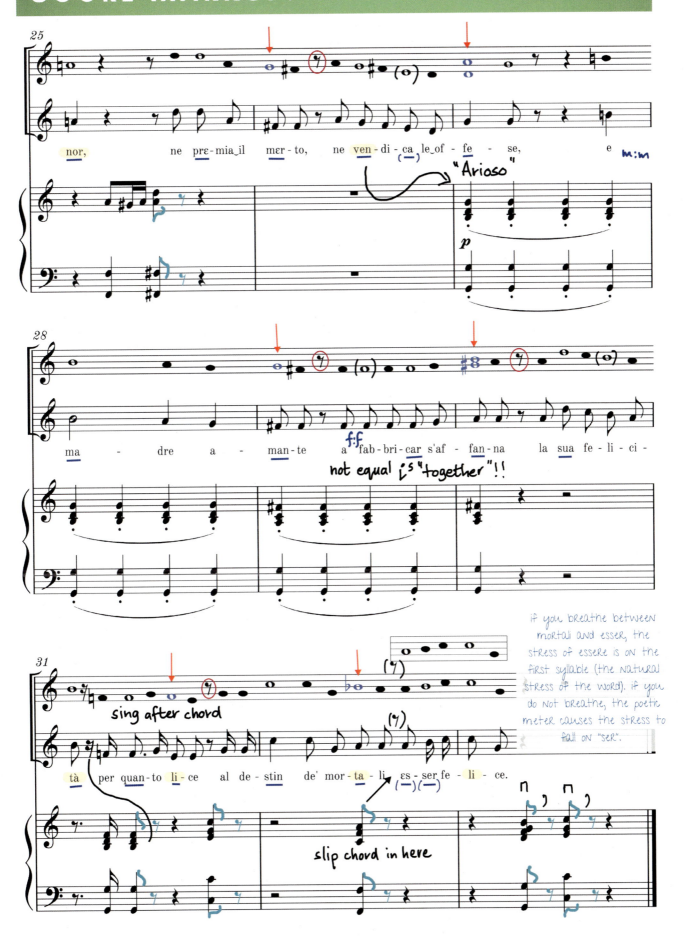

266

Practice Journal

—————— , 20 —

_____

_____

_____

_____

_____

_____

—————— , 20 —

_____

_____

_____

_____

_____

—————— , 20 —

_____

_____

_____

_____

_____

We have historical examples of quite extensive ornamentation in recitative in opera seria where the characters speak with "that decorum with which princes speak, or those who know how to speak to princes." How I love Tosi! If you have not read him, you should. You will fall in love too.

> Il fecondo è Teatrale , che per effer infe-
> parabilmente accompagnato dall'azione del
> Cantante obbliga il Maeftro d'iftruir lo Sco-
> laro d'una certa imitazione naturale , che
> non può effer bella fe non è rapprefentata
> con quel decoro col quale parlano i Princi-
> pi , e quegli che a Principi fanno parlare .

Tosi, *Observations on the Florid Song* (1723)

Here is a mark up where you can compare the original score and an ornamented version of Tancredi's recitative before *Di tanti palpiti*. The ornamented version was written by Rossini for Madame Grégoire on August 15, 1858.

You will see all our old friends (appoggiatura/acciaccatura, passing tones, turns, mordents/neighbor tones) at work as well as dynamic and tempo indications. We cannot all be Rossini, but we can all practice using our ornamentation skills in big presentational monologues like this one.

Our QR code links to a video explaining the parts that were tricky to get on paper.

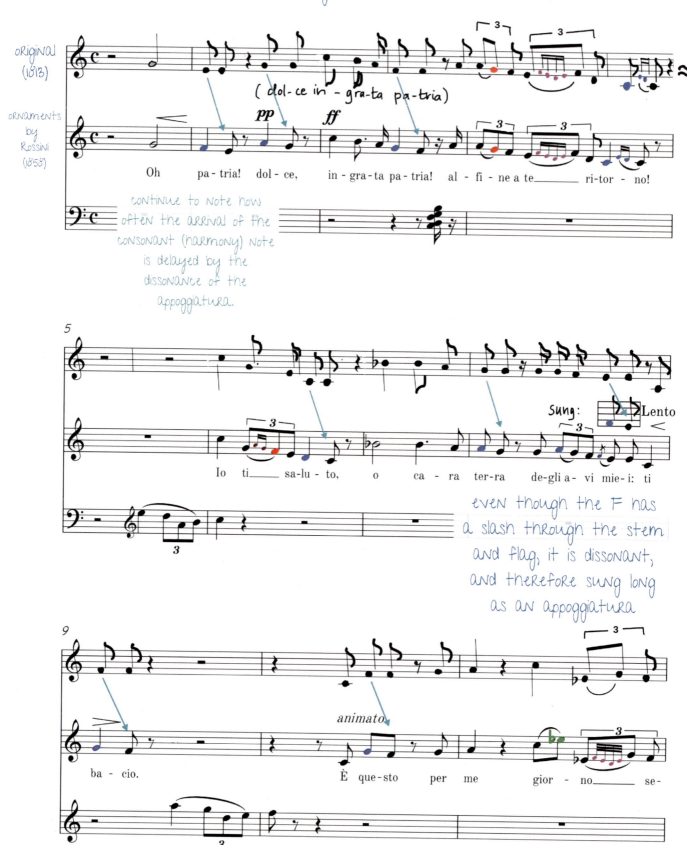

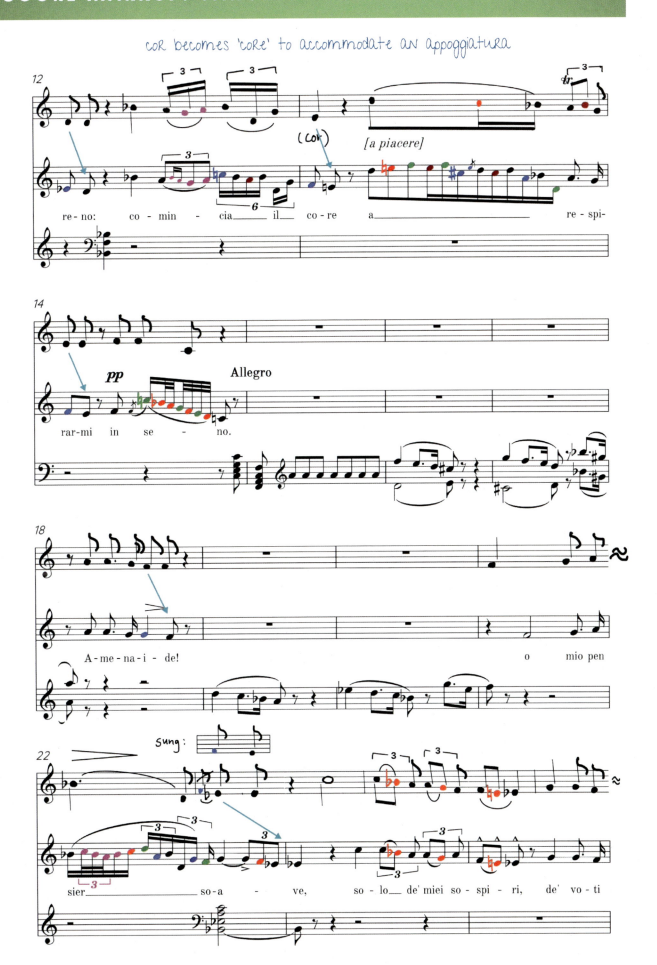

mie - i   ce-le-ste og-get-to,   io

(al - fin)

ven-ni   al - fi - ne: io   vo-glio,   sfi-dan-do il   mio___ de - sti - no,   qua-lun-que si - a,

(o pe- rir)

dolce

me - ri-tar-ti,   o pe - ri - - re,   a - ni - ma mi - a.

Practice Journal

———————— , 20 ——

_____
_____
_____
_____
_____

———————— , 20 ——

_____
_____
_____
_____
_____

———————— , 20 ——

_____
_____
_____
_____
_____
_____

List Recitatives you sing where some ornamentation would be appropriate

_____
_____
_____
_____
_____
_____

Advanced Recitative: Changing Pitches

This chapter is the last application of our lessons learned in Lesson 14. One topic we have not discussed yet is the possibility of **changing the pitches** to carry your intent better. No, the continuo group would not have freaked out! No, you didn't need to tell them in advance! All you needed to do was stick to the same chord progression and arrive at the chord changes on the same prosodic accents as they exist in the score.

After the storm in Rossini's *Il barbiere di Siviglia*, Rosina is upset. I mean, really upset! And she shows it by giving the Count (Lindoro) a piece of her mind. Too often have I heard Rosina strain her voice in an attempt to get her emotion across in a recitative that sits on the low side. There are many other places where a lyric mezzo can help herself in this role by making similar adjustments. But this scene really jumps out as a candidate for this treatment. Giving the voice more scope by singing into the pre-passaggio more often, allows Rosina to express herself without sounding like she wishes her voice were bigger!

Before I hear you thinking "yeah, these recitatives were not by Rossini in any case", let me assure you that that has nothing to do with it. Rossini would not have blinked an eye if you adjusted his very own pitches. He might have blinked an eye if you "Sprechstimmed" your way through this page sounding unelegant, though. Let's avoid that, shall we! Have a look at my solution. How would you tailor it to your own needs?

Remember our previous chapter about ornamentation in Tancredi's monologue? Here is García suggesting some turns and an additional chord tone in the recitative before *Là ci darem la mano*. Some ornamentation is totally permissible in the occasional buffo secco recitative. It does not need to be reserved exclusively for dramatic monologues. One can see how the flirtatious Don Giovanni might add an extra turn or two to his sweet talking of Zerlina. Who can resist a galantly sung turn?!

Are you excited about tackling Lesson 15 next to put it all together? We have very little to tell you!

You have assembled all the skills to unpack scores all on your own!

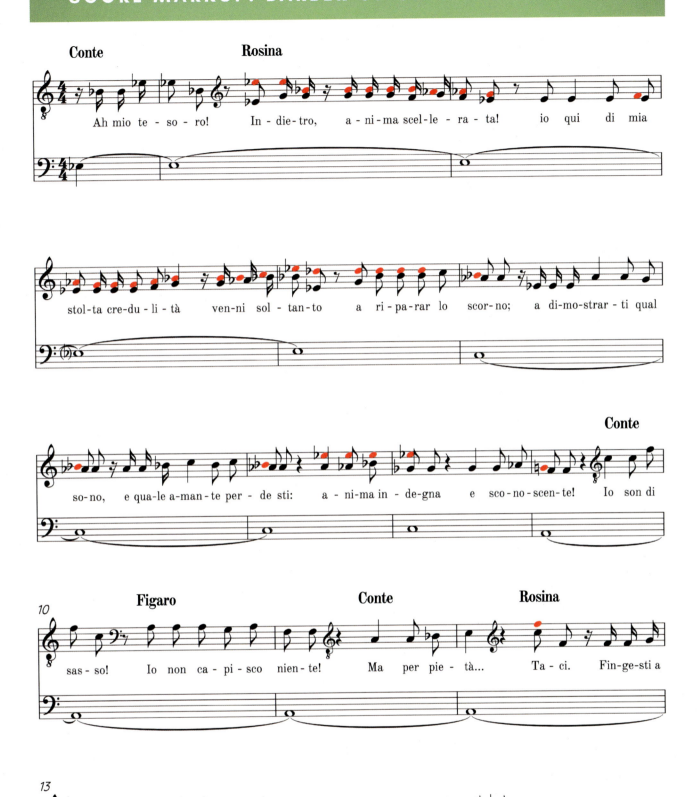

Practice Journal

—————————— , 20 ——

—————————————————————————

—————————————————————————

—————————————————————————

—————————————————————————

—————————————————————————

—————————— , 20 ——

—————————————————————————

—————————————————————————

—————————————————————————

—————————————————————————

—————————————————————————

—————————— , 20 ——

————————————————

————————————————

————————————————

————————————————

————————————————

List recitatives where adjusting the tessitura would help you both vocally and dramatically

————————————————

————————————————

————————————————

————————————————

————————————————

Lezione XV

Riepilogo

15th Lesson

Recapitulation

Moderato

Al - la sta - gion de' fio - ri E de' no - vɛl - li_a - mo - ri, ɛ̀

gra - to_il mɔl - le fia - to D'un zɛ - fi - ro leg -

giɛr, ɛ̀ gra - to il mɔl - le fia - to D'un

zε - - - - fi - ro leg - giεr. O gε - ma, o

gε - ma, o gε - ma tra __ le fron - de, O lεn - to, o

lεn - to, o lεn - to_in - cre - spi __ l'on - de,

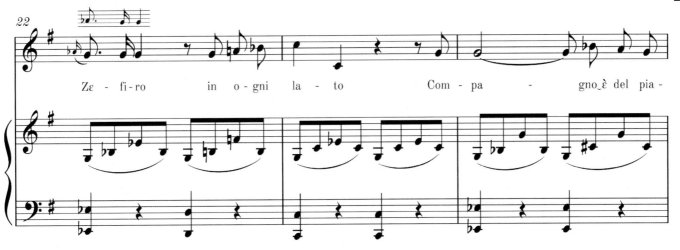

Zε - fi-ro   in o-gni la - to   Com - pa - gno_è del pia-

cer, _____ in o-gni la - to,   in o-gni la - to   Com -

- pa - gno è del pia - cer,   Com - pa-gno, com -

pa-gno, com - - pa - gno_è_____ del pia -

cer, Com - - - pa-gno, com - -

pa - gno, com - - - pa - - - gno_è_____

del pia - cer, è del pia - cer, è del pia -

cer, Com - pa - gno è del_____ pia - cer.

Our final QR code has **Lisette Oropesa** singing our final lesson. This is from the same **Teatro Nuovo Bel Canto in Thirty Minutes** that we visited before with Michael Spyres. Listen to her string together all the skills we practiced during the course with immaculate elegance. You will hear her execute a cadenza by Vaccai at the end of the lesson. See if you can hear the skeleton and which units of pitches Vaccai employed to flesh it out.

Putting It All Together

Can you believe that you have arrived at Lesson 15?! What a fantastic achievement! While the lessons of Vaccai are famous, I'd say they are mostly famous for the lessons up to *Come il candore*. So many singers never venture beyond that, and, if they do, *L'augelletto* brings them to a grinding halt! Not you - you made it all the way here.

When we first did **The Vaccai Project** we actually skipped Lesson 15. There are no new skills to learn here - just application - so we applied our skill set to our every day repertoire. To be honest, I find *Alla stagion de' fiori* the least appealing lesson from a musical perspective. Putting ALL the skills in one musical piece is sure to be just a tad too much - a great recipe has all the needed ingredients, not ALL the ingredients! But, we ran a marathon together and we should cross the finish line together!

Look at Lesson 15 and realize how you don't need us for this. You have learned every lesson to unpack this score for yourself - both libretto and notational conventions. You know why it is written the way it is written.

You can confidently enter into the world implied by the notes on the page.
You can meet the librettist and composer there.
And you can expertly partner with them as you bring the page to life.

Go back to the appropriate lesson to improve a skill if you sing Lesson 15 and get stuck. This is essential, in everything you sing: Do not keep repeating the musical phrase that gives you trouble. Don't even practice it.

PRACTICE THE SKILL THAT IS NOT UP TO SNUFF.
Your repertoire is not the place to improve your technical skill.
YOU KNOW HOW TO DO THIS!

Lesson 15 Grammar

subject	prepositional phrase
verb	interjection
object	conjunction
adjective	interrogative pronoun
adverb	
predicate noun, adv, or adj	

Alla stagion de' fiori
E de' novelli amori
È grato il molle fiato
D' un zefiro leggier.
O gema tra le fronde,
O lento increspi l' onde,
Zefiro in ogni lato
Compagno è del piacer.

You can, and should, consider all your arias and songs to be Lesson 15 of Vaccai and the summary of your work here in **The Vaccai Project**. When you look at your scores you should see the skills jump out at you.

Every needed skill you recognize should conjure up great positive prompts about how you can execute them confidently.

You can trust your technique to unlock your imagination.

Yep, this is a four note turn starting on a non-chord tone — audiate clearly!

Slow cantabile piece!

Time to show off my impeccable legato!

Ornamentation time! I'VE GOT THIS!

Wait... two of the same pitches before a rest... definitely must place an appoggiatura!

Double m:m — going to keep my one breath impulse going through that consonant!

While I'm at it... let me look through this whole piece and find and practice all my sustainable double consonants.

DONE!!

mmmm... D4... should probably sing this in chest to improve my color palette

Gonna sing the hell out of this coloratura! UNITS OF PITCHES FTW!

YOU DID IT! We are so proud of you for completing this course!

Practice Journal

——————— , 20 —

_____

_____

_____

_____

_____

_____

——————— , 20 —

_____

_____

_____

_____

_____

——————— , 20 —

_____

_____

_____

_____

_____

Made in the USA
Columbia, SC
11 May 2022